New York University School of Law
Series in Legal History
Board of Editors

Linden Studies in Legal History

The Linden studies in legal history, honoring Bella L. Linden, have been established by New York University School of Law, in appreciation of her contributions to the School, and by her friends, in recognition of her distinguished service at the New York bar.

New York University School of Law
Series in Legal History: 4

Harmony & Dissonance:

The *Swift* & *Erie* Cases in American Federalism

Tony Freyer

Linden Studies in American Legal History

New York University Press • New York and London
1981

Library of Congress Cataloging in Publication Data

Freyer, Tony Allan.
  Harmony & dissonance.

  (New York University School of Law series in legal history. Linden studies in American legal history; 2)
  Includes bibliographical references and index.
  1. Judicial power—United States. 2. Judicial review—United States. 3. Federal government—United States. 4. Common law—United States. I. Title. II. Title: History and dissonance. III. Series.
KF5130.F74   347.73'202   81-9614
ISBN 0-8147-2568-6   347.30712   AACR2

Manufactured in the United States of America

Contents

Preface

Many have contributed in different ways to the writing of this book. Morton J. Horwitz suggested the subject; his course in the fall of 1975 brought to my attention the broader social dimension implicit in the story. Harry N. Scheiber has supported the project over the years and aided significantly in its completion in the present form. I owe a continuing debt to Bernard Sheehan, Morris Arnold, Irene Neu, and Maurice Baxter who helped me during the early stages of the project. Edward Sherman and Miss Betty LeBuss also rendered kind and invaluable assistance early on. Portions of this study could not have been written without the help of Glenn Porter, Fritz Redlich, and Alfred D. Chandler, Jr. and the financial support of the Newcomen Society of North America and the Harvard Business School.

I gratefully acknowledge the superb resources of the Harvard Law School Library, the excellent service of Morris Cohen's staff, and use of office space during the summer of 1978. Miss Edith Henderson was most helpful on several occasions. I owe a special debt to Mrs. Erika Chadbourn and her assistant in manuscripts, whose friendly and skillful work is matched only by the quality of the collection they have built up. I appreciate also permission given by Professors Paul Freund and Grant Gilmore to use the papers of Justice Holmes, Justice Brandeis, and Felix Frankfurter.

I experienced the pleasure of several rewarding interviews with Professors Robert A. Leflar, David Cavers, Austin W. Scott, Louis Luski, and Mr. Aaron Danzig. Former clerks of Mr. Justice Brandeis, including Professors Freund and Willard Hurst, Honorable Judge Henry J. Friendly, and W. Graham Claytor, Jr., secretary of the navy also gave generously of their time.

The assistance of Professors Robert Foster and Frank Stites was also helpful. I am indebted to the excellent scholarship of Professor Irving Younger. After working on the record of *Erie* I encountered Professor Younger's superb study of the litigation and found to my dismay that I could not improve upon it. It is used here with his kind permission. Colleagues Thomas Kaiser and Charles Bolton have been supportive. I recognize also the aid of C. Fred Williams, a chairman who has done what he could to foster research. Others who have rendered essential service on different occasions are Professors Melvin I. Urofsky, Bruce Murphy, Charles McCurdy, and Mr. Richard Butler. Mrs. F. R. Hodgson, Brandeis project archivist, University Archives & Record Center, University of Louisville has been helpful too. I appreciate also the willingness of Mr. Justice William J. Brennan to respond to inquiries.

Much of the research for this project would have been impossible without the generous support of the American Bar Foundation and the National Endowment for the Humanities. Travel grants from the American Philosophical Society and the University of Arkansas at Little Rock facilitated completion of the interviews.

The aid of the library staff of the University of Arkansas at Little Rock and of the Law School of Tulane University is also gratefully acknowledged.

Mr. Christopher Jones contributed valuable assistance as a copy editor. Rhonda Reagan gave friendly, skillful, and timely service in typing the endless drafts. Nancy Moyers and Debra Bowers typed portions of the manuscript also.

Material included here appeared in the *Business History Review* and other published work.

The interest of Harold Hyman, who suggested the project, is gratefully acknowledged. William E. Nelson has been of invaluable assistance in shaping several portions of the study. The remarks of the anonymous reader were also helpful.

The assistance of others does not, of course, affect my responsibility for what has been written.

Finally, and of most importance, I dedicate the results to Allan, a nineteen-month-old son who made it possible for his father to keep life's priorities straight during several difficult months.

December 1979   Tony Freyer
Wilmington, Delaware

Introduction

Questions of federal jurisdiction, for many people involve no more than the application of technical formulae created only to confuse the uninitiated. More sophisticated students of government understand that these problems involve fundamental questions of power, and that the existence of democracy depends in no small part upon the allocation of such authority.

Philip B. Kurland, "Mr. Justice Frankfurter," 1957

The federal government's authority has become, in the last third of the twentieth century, fundamental to our society. Until the end of the nineteenth century, however, it was the government of the states which had the greatest influence over the lives of most Americans. The shift in the center of power from the state to the national government was part of a major transformation in the character of American federalism. Essential to this shift has been the change in the limits of power of legal institutions over individuals. This study examines a small but important part of this transformation: the changing nature of the federal judiciary's authority over state law in disputes involving private rights. The focus of this work will be two leading, controversial Supreme Court decisions, *Swift* v. *Tyson* decided in 1842 and *Erie* v. *Tompkins* decided in 1938.

In the *Swift* case, the Supreme Court held that federal judges were free to apply their own discretion in determining the rule of decision in common law litigation, irrespective of state law. Ninety-six years later the *Erie* opinion reversed *Swift*, proclaiming that the earlier decision was an invalid usurpation of state power. The *Erie* decision

brought about a significant alteration in the relations between federal and state courts. By the 1970s however, it was
unclear whether this alteration was consistent with the original intent of the opinion. A large commentary on these decisions has been confined generally to textual comparisons
and analysis of cases. With a few noted exceptions, little attempt has been made to consider either or both of these
cases in a broader social context. An examination of the
Swift and *Erie* cases not only in terms of the evolution of
doctrine, but also as part of changing social milieu involving
the legal profession, political confrontation in Congress,
business interests, jurisprudential thinking, localism, and
the judicial process, may contribute to our understanding
of the role of law and legal institutions in American society.

Judicial review and other issues concerning the role of
the Supreme Court in interpreting the Constitution have
been the focus of many studies of the federal judiciary. But
the great bulk of the cases litigated in federal courts have
involved relatively mundane, though nonetheless socially
important, questions such as debtor-creditor relations, accident liability, property transfers, and other matters of private right. Until the mid-twentieth century (when state and
federal legislation became dominant) courts were the institutions most responsible for adjudicating questions of private right on the basis of the common law. Due to the private character of this litigation, the judges' application of
common-law rules could have significant social impact.
Thus, the determination of the appropriate jurisdiction of
federal and state courts in the administration of the common law carried important implications for the lives of individuals and whole communities, as well as the power of
federal and state government.

The Supreme Court's decision in *Swift* v. *Tyson* meant in
effect that federal judges were free to determine for themselves the common-law rules governing private litigation, irregardless of the local law. This independent judgment had
two major consequences. First, it fostered a condition in
which two different versions of the common law might be

administered in the same jurisdiction. Second, it gave federal judges the means to develop a common law that was not only different from state law but also more favorable to the interests of those resorting to the national tribunals. Admittance to federal court until the middle of the twentieth century (with few important exceptions) depended upon the diversity of citizenship of parties to the suit. Throughout the nineteenth century, out-of-state creditors experienced difficulty in recovering debts from local debtors because of uncertainty and even outright prejudice evident in state law. Due to a combination of diversity jurisdiction and the *Swift* doctrine, however, these creditors sued in federal court because federal judges very often applied the common law on behalf of creditor rights.

By the first third of the twentieth century a body of federal "general law" had evolved that tended to favor the interests of interstate business. The *Erie* decision held that the formulation of this general law constituted an unconstitutional usurpation of state power. A central thesis of this study will be that the theory of *Erie* v. *Tompkins* rests upon a perception of federal judicial authority over the common law which evolved in the late nineteenth century, a view which cannot, therefore, be appropriately applied to the *Swift* decision. An examination of the origin of the *Swift* litigation in the colorful and complex commercial transactions of two Maine speculators and the members of a New York City company will be the starting point of discussion. These transactions used standard mercantile contracts of the period; the case, therefore, raised issues vital to the whole antebellum mercantile order. An analysis of the trial and decision of *Swift* that considers the relationship of this business order to the functioning of the antebellum credit system, the role of the federal courts in this system, the character of the legal profession during the period, and prevalent jurisprudential assumptions concerning the nature of law and the federal system, should establish a basis for the argument that *Swift* was thoroughly consistent with antebellum notions of American constitutionalism and federalism.

The *Swift* doctrine underwent a transformation as it evolved from the 1840s to 1900. Beginning in the 1870s the doctrine and its relationship to diversity jurisdiction became the object of heated debate in Congress and generated a divergence of opinion among members of the legal profession. Critics in Congress sought to weaken the growing power of national corporate business by obliterating the *Swift* principle and limiting federal jurisdiction. The motivation behind the bar's resistance was more complex, involving developments in legal education, concern for preserving the public image of the legal profession, and changes in jurisprudential thinking that ultimately became associated with positivism. Occasionally federal judges and justices of the Supreme Court dissented in particular cases applying *Swift,* but these objections were spasmodic. On the whole, this criticism was vocal but not widespread before the turn of the century; its influence increased, however, because of the teaching and writing of several prominent legal scholars.

The work of these scholars, coupled with the general concern for the rise of big business and government centralization, were the chief sources of the theory of federalism written into the *Erie* decision. During the early twentieth century this critical tradition gained the support of many prominent teachers of law and members of the bar. At the same time, a significant minority of the Supreme Court, lead by Justice Oliver Wendell Holmes, formed a fairly consistent block of dissenters. In 1934 an accident involving an unemployed laborer gave the Supreme Court the opportunity to reevaluate the *Swift* precedent in light of a critical tradition that had developed over more than half a century. The decision of 1938, then, was the culmination of this development, a conclusion substantiated by an examination of the drafting of the opinion itself.

Since 1938 the federal system of which *Erie* was a cornerstone underwent a fundamental transformation. Following the New Deal the federal government increasingly overlapped or displaced the authority of the states as the dominant force in the private lives of most Americans. The intent of *Erie* was to bind federal courts to state law; but as centralization increased, the jurisdiction governed by the doctrine shrunk. At the same time a new federal common law evolved derived from federal statutes and regulations. Under *Swift* a general law had evolved, but (with rare exceptions) state courts were free to develop their own jurisprudence as it applied to local residents. The new federal common law, however, bound state tribunals because it was extrapolated from federal law and was therefore supreme. Thus by the 1970s centralization threatened to overturn the decentralist intent of the *Erie* opinion; lawyers and judges wrestled with the implications of this for the preservation of American federalism under the Constitution.

Harmony & Dissonance:

The *Swift* & *Erie* Cases
in American Federalism

Chapter I

The Swift Case

Nothing in law springs entirely from a sense of convenience. There are always certain ideas existing antecedently on which the sense of convenience works, and of which it can do no more than form some new combination; and to find these ideas is exactly the problem.

Sir Henry Maine, *Ancient Law*

THE PROBLEM

Justice Louis D. Brandeis wrote the majority opinion in *Erie R.R.* v. *Tompkins*. Although the opinion was ambiguous on several points, its refutation of *Swift* was clear. Brandeis argued forcefully that the 96-year-old precedent rested upon a false theory. This theory held, the justice said, that there was a general law independent of and separate from the jurisprudence of the states. But there was no such law, Brandeis affirmed, and resort to this erroneous principle usurped state authority and violated fundamental tenets of American constitutionalism. Brandeis' views concerning general law provided the basis for what became after 1938 the dominant interpretation of *Swift* v. *Tyson*.[1]

The *Erie* reading of *Swift* (like *Swift* itself) has been the subject of much discussion and criticism. One of the most insightful critics of the Brandeis interpretation has been Morton J. Horwitz. As early as the 1820s, Horwitz argued, American judges had moved away from notions of law based upon what Holmes had called some "brooding omnipresence in the sky." After the turn of the century, antebel-

1

lum judges increasingly used legal rules to facilitate economic and social change. Given the triumph of this instrumental conception of jurisprudence, how could the court in *Swift* have relied upon a "general law"? Horwitz concluded that the language of general law was in reality a formalistic device used to mask more utilitarian purposes. These purposes involved efforts at formulating a body of rules favorable to national commercial interests and development, irrespective of state law.[2]

Despite this and other scholarship, the meaning of *Swift* remains obscure. One source of confusion involves the controversy over a federal common law of crimes. Draftsmen of the Constitution and the Judiciary Act of 1789 (the statute that established the original structure of the federal judicial system) probably intended that federal judges should have the authority to fashion rules of criminal law in the absence of federal statute and in spite of state law. There was, however, no clear provision in either document or later process acts giving such power. Federal courts in the 1790s assumed the authority, but with the passage of the Alien and Sedition Acts this policy came under heated Jeffersonian attack. Since the enforcement of these acts required federal judges to develop what amounted to a common law of crimes, federal jurisdiction threatened, Jeffersonians claimed, constitutional principles of limited federal power. Agitation over the issue continued until 1816 when a divided Supreme Court disavowed any authority to create a federal criminal law in *United States* v. *Coolidge*.[3]

The intensity of this controversy, with its sensitive political implications, raises questions concerning *Swift*. The decision in 1842 was unanimous. Joining in this unanimity was a majority of Jacksonian Democrats who shared the values and political persuasion of the Jeffersonian critics of a federal criminal common law. Although *Swift* dealt expressly with commercial issues, its assertion of a general law claimed an authority to ignore state jurisprudence similar to that denied in *United States* v. *Coolidge*. How could a majority of Jacksonian judges, including such Democratic stalwarts as Chief Justice Roger B. Taney and Justice Peter V. Daniel, agree unanimously with an opinion written by the nationalist Joseph Story?[4]

Perplexing enough in its own right, this question confuses further the proposition underlying the *Erie* decision and also challenges the view that *Swift* represented a formalistic device designed to defeat state prerogatives in favor of national business interests. How could Peter Daniel—who has been characterized as the most extreme states' rights enthusiast ever to sit on the Supreme Court—have concurred in so significant an extension of federal jurisdiction? How could this Virginia planter—who dissented in virtually every attempt to extend federal jurisdiction over corporations and other agents of a new mercantile order—have accepted *Swift* if it was in fact an engine of national commercial power?[5]

Edwin D. Dickinson of the University of Pennsylvania school of law gave a partial answer to these questions. Dickinson argued that *Swift* did not fundamentally involve questions of federal-state relations; rather, the decision applied widely accepted notions concerning courts' jurisdiction over commercial law. This meant that federal and state judges assumed as a premise of jurisprudential thinking that there were cases in which local law must govern as well as those in which principles of "universal law" applied. Dickinson noted that political controversies, such as those involving the federal common law of crimes, narrowed the federal judiciary's jurisdiction over this universal law. The idea, however, that federal and state courts were free to apply "universal" commercial principles in appropriate cases remained a foundation of American legal thought until the Civil War.[6]

According to Dickinson, then, the central issue in *Swift* involved merely a fairly straightforward application of commercial law. "This was what the court decided," he said, "and all that it decided." The law professor admitted that there was "unnecessary" and "confused" language in the decision which complicated its meaning for later courts. But this should not, he argued, obscure the extent to which a conception of commercial jurisprudence—rather than federalism—was the main point in the case. As will become apparent, there was during the early nineteenth century more ambiguity in the jurisprudential underpinnings of the idea of a general commercial law than Dickinson said. His argument remains important, however, because it moves analysis away from the line of reasoning suggested in *Erie* toward a more fruitful course of inquiry.[7]

But if neither federalism nor national commerce were the central questions in *Swift*, what *was* the main issue? Tracing the evolution and eventual decision of the *Swift* case within the context of several interrelated themes suggests an answer to this question. A major theme involves an understanding of the role of the federal judiciary in the operation of national business before the Civil War. Throughout the antebellum period, federal courts were conceived of as alternative forums to the tribunals of the states. An alternative to state courts was necessary in order that nonresidents might have the means to avoid the uncertainties and sporadic prejudices of local law. Federal judges had carried out this role in commercial litigation since the 1790s. By 1840, however, it was apparent that confusion in jurisprudential thinking concerning the source of commercial principles of law threatened the federal judiciary's traditional function. It was clear that the Supreme Court must formulate a rule that would ameliorate this confusion for federal judges, while also preserving the authority of the state courts. The decision of *Swift* v. *Tyson* may be understood in terms of the Court's effort to achieve this dual purpose.[8]

SWIFT *AND ANTEBELLUM BUSINESS*

The *Swift* case originated during the mid-1830s in several intricate credit transactions between two residents of Maine and a group of businessmen in New York City. Jarius Keith and Nathaniel Norton were active land speculators in Penobscot County (a remote area with great development potential in northeastern Maine). Some time in 1835 the two associates were approached with an offer to sell a large tract in the northern county by an agent of the European, who owned it. In order to make the deal, Keith and Norton concocted a scheme to raise money through a questionable (probably illegal) manipulation of commercial credit. Through a contact in New York, a company was formed whose members were led to believe that they were purchasing the land directly from Norton and Keith. Actually, the men from Maine used the installments paid them by the New Yorkers to make regular payments to the European's agent. This transfer of credit was made possible by the negotiation of numerous promissory notes and bills of exchange. The scheme, and the contracts made in carrying it through, collapsed with the disruption of credit following the Panic of 1837. Keith and Norton declared their insolvency, and the New York company learned of the questionable legality of the entire transaction.[9]

The members of the company let it become "common knowledge on Wall Street" that they would not cover the commercial contracts. One who had been involved in the scheme—George W. Tysen—was unable to escape obligation, however. As part of the larger transaction, Tysen had signed and accepted a bill of exchange which had been drawn by Keith and Norton. This bill eventually came into the hands of Joseph Swift, but under rather questionable and complicated circumstances. Keith and Norton paid off a creditor in Maine with a promissory note. The creditor cashed the note at his bank, which then passed it along to Keith's and Norton's bank in Portland. The cashier of the Portland bank was Swift, who failed to cover the note when it became due. When the creditor's bank demanded payment, Swift's failure came to light. The cashier covered the note from his own funds and then went to Norton demanding payment. Norton paid off Swift by endorsing to him the bill of exchange that had been accepted by Tysen. With this endorsement Tysen became indebted to Swift.

Whether in fact, however, Tysen would ever pay the debt was a difficult question. Swift's failure to cover the original note suggested the possibility of collusion between the cashier and the two insolvent businessmen. But even if there were no illegal dealings involved, the respective rights and obligations of Swift and Tysen were clouded by several business and legal realities. The legal problems involved the commercial principle of negotiability, the principle by which bills and notes were legally transferred from one person to another. While the law of most states sanctioned this principle in general, there was a great diversity among the states as to whether particular instruments were indeed negotiable. A major point of dispute involved whether those to whom bills had been endorsed possessed an absolute right of recovery against debtors, even where the possibility of fraud existed. This concerned directly the rights of Swift against Tysen. There was little doubt that fraud was involved in the original drawing of the bill by Keith and Norton and its acceptance by Tysen. There was also possible collusion between Swift and Norton. Should the law give an absolute right of recovery to those in Swift's position, irregardless of the possible presence of fraud?[10]

This question divided state courts in part because it carried vital implications for the conduct of domestic and international business. It was often extremely difficult to determine whether in fact a particular credit transaction involved fraud. This was true not only in cases involving speculation, but also for those ordinary business exchanges carried on throughout the mercantile world. The character of the credit instruments used in both speculation and regular business was exactly the same. Thus it was hard (sometimes impossible) to establish clear rules governing the principle of negotiability. But the principle was essential to antebellum business.[11]

Due in part to the degree of certainty which the doctrine of negotiability brought to business transactions, wholesalers in the East extended credit to farmers and shopkeepers in the West and South, exchanging merchandise for crops while expecting payment after the season harvest. The South's cotton economy also depended on the endorsement of bills and notes between the planter's factors and American and English banks. Since the antebellum economy suffered a chronic scarcity of specie and lacked a uniform currency, credit transactions using negotiable instruments served as the leading circulating medium for most long-distance transfers of capital and credit. Thus, the status of Swift's rights against Tysen raised an issue involving the effective operation of the entire mercantile order.

Along with the economic considerations raised by Swift's standing as a creditor, were other less obvious but important concerns involving the interests of a particular social group. This group included specialized middlemen who had come to dominate the American economy by the 1830s and 40s. From the colonial period to the War of 1812, general, all-purpose merchants living in the seaport towns of Boston, New York, Philadelphia, Baltimore, Charleston, and Savannah strongly influenced America's social and economic life. These individuals were called general merchants because they handled all facets of commerce. They traded in a great variety of goods in markets all over the world and were engaged in a wide range of commercial activities including shipping, insurance, wholesaling and retailing, importing, and exporting.

The uncertainties generated by the Napoleonic Wars, the Embargo, and finally the British blockade facilitated the preeminence of the general merchant until the cessation of hostilities in 1815. Only a relatively few wealthy individuals could bear the cost of disrupted and distorted international commerce. But peace and the Treaty of Ghent in 1815 freed the United States from these internal and external liabilities and brought the nation to the verge of a dramatic economic transformation. The general merchants who had dominated American business since the colonial period gradually lost their influence and leadership to a new class of specialized businessmen. This transformation from general to specialized merchant was not based upon a change in goods, the appearance of new markets, or alterations in the kinds of services to be performed by merchants. The fundamental change bringing about increased specialization was a great expansion in the volume of goods traded in domestic and foreign markets.

As long as volume remained comparatively small, the all-purpose merchant could handle every facet of the transactions necessary for the buying, distribution, and selling of his goods. As the volume of trade increased, a merchant could now have a large volume business in the area he knew best, or which presented the greatest return; in addition, the number of transactions increased as well. Thus the merchant adapted to changes brought about by increased volume by specializing in either a particular commodity or trading function. And as greater specialization brought ever increasing numbers of credit transactions, the law's relationship to these factors became still more important. A writer for *Hunt's* hinted at this in 1846. "The mercantile connection has become so intimate and so vast, and is still so rapidly increasing, between great commercial cities of the North and those of the South," he said, "that some knowledge of the rights and duties, and liabilities, of merchants . . . has become a matter of real necessity, to the safe and prosperous conduct of business affairs."[12]

But if the law governing commercial contracts was essential to the merchant's business, it was also fraught with uncertainty. In a "community possessing a great and diversified commerce composed of people who push their enterprise into every possible sphere," remarked a commentator for *Hunt's* in 1842, "even the laws of their own creating, to meet the vast variety of cases that will arise, and the changes which time effects in their trade and habits, must necessarily become voluminous, intricate, and frequently . . . conflicting."[13] The dependency of the "mercantile community," said another observer in the same periodical some years later, on the "discordant legislation" of the different states makes "some knowledge of the general principles of these different systems almost indispensable to the proper management of business." This uncertainty in legal rules created by the law of distinct and separate state jurisdictions was particularly distressing to middlemen in the large commercial cities. These matters were, the same writer remarked, "emphatically interesting to importers and dealers in our large cities—the creditors, whose rights and duties are constantly subject to such various construction and control."[14]

There were many reasons for this uncertainty. As will become apparent, some of these arose out of antebellum America's jurisprudence. Others involved the complex or questionable practices pursued by merchants, such as those carried on by Keith, Norton, and the New York partnership. No doubt another important source of confusion was the persistent rivalry among urban business centers. This rivalry could not help but create suspicion between local and out-of-state merchants, as the New Yorker's refusal to honor the bills of exchange suggested. Add to these the underdeveloped character of credit reporting agencies and we see a national business environment fraught with uncertainty throughout. But behind these factors were two vague, but nonetheless vital, notions representing a significant antimercantile tradition in the nation's history. The first notion was a general distrust of credit and "soft money" of all kinds, evidenced by a critic writing for *Hunt's* in 1839. "CREDIT, CREDIT,—with very little regard to the means of paying,—often ruinous to both parties is the fatal bane of commercial prosperity, of commercial honor and honesty. The transactions of business are little more than fictions."[15]

The second notion reflected a distinct cleavage between mercantile and agrarian businessmen. A Georgian, one Benjamin F. Porter, stated this assumption plainly in *Hunt's*. "We have had occasion, very often of late," said Porter, "to observe with much concern, that a deep-rooted prejudice is entertained by the agriculturalists against the mercantile class. Among the former, indeed, is to be found a general distrust of commercial men." The reasons for this, Porter continued (and here again we are reminded of the extent to which the basic forms of Keith's and Norton's dealings applied to legitimate commercial enterprise of the period) were not hard to find. Merchants "are regarded as sharpers, whose lives are spent in acquiring a knowledge of arts by which to deceive the producer;—as men who live upon that class; who exist not by labor, but by swindling and ingenuity;—as drones of society, consuming the results of the toil of others, and yielding nothing whatever to the community in which they live."[16]

Concerning the principle of negotiability, this plethora of factors often contributed to a marked uncertainty in legal rules. The status of bills received in payment of preexisting debts illustrated such uncertainty. This is a useful example because it describes the circumstances under which Swift acquired the bill of exchange from Norton. Recall that Norton endorsed the bill to Swift in payment for another debt originally contracted between another creditor and the two Maine speculators. The earlier debt, was "preexisting" or "antecedent" to the debt for which Norton was paying Swift (who had already paid the other creditor from his personal funds). The intricacies of such transactions raised a complex legal question: Did the holders of bills received for antecedent debts qualify as bonafide creditors? This was a difficult question because of the requirements which had to be met in order to qualify as such a creditor. These requirements stated that the holder of a bill must have received it in the due course of trade for a valuable consideration. Under old common-law rules, a preexisting debt was not a "valuable consideration," and a bill given in payment for such a debt was not received in the "due course of business." According to Lord Mansfield's commercial doctrines, however, these bills *did* qualify their holders as bona fide creditors and were therefore negotiable.[17]

Conditions in New York suggested how tangled the question of preexisting debts could become. In 1821, in *Bay* v. *Coddington,* Chancellor James Kent refused to extend the negotiability principle to certain forms of commercial paper involving fraud. In doing so, however, he *did* admit (though only indirectly) that bills received in payment of preexisting debts were negotiable. Perhaps because of Kent's oblique recognition of preexisting debts having value, later New York judges in the common-law courts misread *Bay* v. *Coddington* and decided that bills held for antecedent debts did not guarantee their holders an absolute right of recovery. In 1837, the reporter of the New York decision, *Smith* v. *Van Loan* (which followed a true reading of Kent's decision), acknowledged that the question was "unsettled" in the state's local law but that the "weight of authority" favored giving those holding bills received for preexisting debts the rights of a bona fide holder.[18] Soon, the New York Supreme Court upheld the same principle in two banking cases (though the doctrine remained in dispute until the twentieth century).[19]

This was the status of the principle of negotiability in New York law when Swift sued Tysen in the spring of 1837. After a futile attempt to settle out of court, Swift's attorney, Thomas Fessenden (a leading Portland lawyer), initiated suit in the Federal Court of the Southern District of New York. The defendant's lawyer was Alexander Hope Dana, a well-known and successful New York attorney, writer of influential legal treatises, and distant relative of the Danas of Massachusetts. To counter Fessenden's efforts, Dana asked the federal court for an injunction, and then filed on the equity side of the court a bill of discovery through which he hoped to uncover evidence that would weaken or destroy Swift's case. The court issued the injunction and ordered discovery proceedings.[20]

For nearly a year after the injunction, Swift collected evidence and supplied affidavits to the federal district judge in Maine, in accord with the process initiated under the bill of discovery. Through this process Dana sought to gather proof showing that Swift was in collusion with Keith and Norton. In doing so, he hoped to lay the basis for an argument that Swift had been involved in a probable fraud and did not, therefore, have the defenses of a bonafide creditor.

The discovery process uncovered no conclusive proof of any connection between Swift and the drawers of the bill of exchange. It also revealed how cloudy were the facts surrounding Tysen's acceptance of the bill and its endorsement to Swift. This led to the two questions upon which the case would ultimately turn: Did the bill come into Swift's hands with no knowledge on his part of any fraud in its making? Did he receive the bill in the "regular course of trade" or had he in fact been working with Keith and Norton? With these questions at issue the injunction was dissolved and the case of *Swift* v. *Tysen* was heard by Judge Samuel R. Betts before a jury.

Fessenden's case depended on whether he could prevent the introduction of evidence that might impeach Swift's standing as a bona fide creditor. Dana's argument aimed to undermine Swift's status by contending that Tysen retained defenses against fraud that released him from obligation to cover the bill. Despite Fessenden's efforts, Betts time and again ruled in favor of Dana and finally instructed the jury in terms that resulted in a verdict for Tysen. The jury's decision did not, however, stop Fessenden. There was good reason to believe that upon appeal another result might be possible, since the facts in the case were after all quite obscure. If, in a new trial, another court could be convinced to instruct the jury under principles favoring the principle of negotiability, Swift might yet win. Fessenden may have been encouraged by the fact that New York precedents (upon which Betts had perhaps relied) were in fact contradictory concerning the rights of those in Tysen's position.

Swift's attorney appealed the *Swift* case late in the winter of 1839 to the Federal Circuit Court for the Southern District of New York. The appeal took place amidst the deepening panic and depression of 1837–1843. Fessenden argued the case before Betts and Smith Thompson, associate justice of the United States Supreme Court. The circuit courts were unique in that a visiting Supreme Court justice joined the federal district judge in hearing appeals. Often, however, one or the other judge was unable to sit, creating the remarkable situation in which the judge hearing the appeal may have also presided over the trial stage of the case. The record of the *Swift* litigation presents an incomplete statement of counsel's argument before the circuit court. It does show that during the initial stages of the appeal, Fessenden and Dana debated the disputable facts of how Swift received the bill, of Tysen's acceptance, and of the probable fraud carried out by Keith and Norton.

But sometime during the argument, a new and important dimension was introduced into the case—the question "arose" whether section 34 of the Judiciary Act of 1789 was relevant to the case. The section read: "That the laws of the several states, except where the constitution, treaties or statues of the United States shall otherwise require or provide, shall be regarded as rules of decision in trials of common law in the courts of the United States in cases where they apply." Did these words bind the federal court to instruct juries, or make rules of decision, only according to the local law? Did the section mean that the appeals court must uphold Betts' instructions to the jury (which followed one line of a confused series of New York precedents)?[21]

Although the record says little about what happened, it does show that Betts and Thompson could not agree on how to apply section 34. Thompson would not accept Betts' opinion that local New York law should govern the court's opinion. During the nation's early years, disagreements of this sort were appealed to the Supreme Court on a certificate of division for clarification. So *Swift* went to the high court early in 1840. Daniel Webster argued the appeal on Swift's side while Dana apparently argued for Tysen. The Supreme Court then demanded further argument, and Chief Justice Taney sent the issue back to the circuit court. Again the record is silent on what happened, but sometime in late 1841 the case went back to the Supreme Court for a final hearing.

Dana and Fessenden argued the *Swift* case during its final appeal before the Supreme Court in January 1842. Fessenden stressed first the extent to which the question of negotiability was vital to the operation of the nation's mercantile order. "If there is any question of law, not local, but widely general in its nature and effects," he exclaimed, "it is the present question. It is one in which foreigners, the citizens of different states . . . nay, every nation of the civilized commercial world, are deeply interested."[22] Swift's lawyer then turned to section 34. As far as his client's case was concerned, he said, the question posed by the section was whether to follow the confused New York precedents or the Mansfieldian principle of negotiability.

The determination of this question depended on the meaning of the word *laws*. Fessenden claimed that the language in section 34 bound federal judges to follow local law only in cases involving state statutes. In "popular" usage the attorney said, "laws" and statutes were the same thing; the meaning of the word did not include local customs and other common-law rules. There was, of course, no statute in New York that regulated the principle of negotiability raised in the *Swift* case. Instead, Fessenden stressed, there was only a jumble of contradictory court opinions pertaining to the subject. Following this narrow construction of section 34 the Supreme Court was not bound to follow the New York opinions since they were not "laws." Where, then, should the Court look for a rule to govern the case, if not in the local law of the state? Where else, Fessenden concluded, but to the "general commercial law," the law of "all commercial nations."[23]

Dana did not dispute the issue of negotiability. He devoted his argument to the "proper" construction of section 34 and the word *laws*. Except for federal statutes, treaties and the Constitution itself, the only law federal judges could follow to settle cases was, Dana said, the law of the different states. The New York attorney admitted that controversy surrounded the meaning of section 34. Writers of legal treatises and state and federal judges had been unable to agree upon the precise meaning of that section. It was time, therefore, Tysen's lawyer argued, for the Supreme Court to end the controversy once and for all. The importance of the question was such, said Dana, that "it may not be supererogatory to examine it anew; as the question is now presented in a form that calls for a specific and final decision of the whole matter."[24]

The opinion of the Court was written by Joseph Story. The justice considered first the New York decisions and their standing in federal court under section 34. He concluded that "[i]n the ordinary use of language it will hardly be contended that the decisions of courts constitute laws. They are, at most," Story said, "only evidence of what the laws are, and are not themselves laws." The New York decisions, he added, were merely deduced from "general principles" of the commercial law. The judge then construed section 34 as "limited [in] its application to state laws strictly local; that is to say, to the positive statutes of the state, and the construction thereof adopted by the local tribunals, and to rights and titles to real estate, and other matters immovable and intraterritorial in their nature and character."[25]

In questions concerning general commercial law, the federal courts did not consider section 34 controlling. The federal courts, like the state courts, followed their own discretion in ascertaining the appropriate commercial principle. "It was never supposed by us," said Story, "that the section did apply . . . to questions of a more general nature, not at all dependent upon local statutes, or local usages of a fixed and permanent operation, as . . . to the construction of ordinary contracts or other written instruments, and especially to questions of general commercial law." The state courts did the same, the justice said, "when called upon to perform the like function . . . to ascertain upon general reasoning and legal analogies, what is the true exposition of the contract, or instrument, or what is the rule furnished by the principles of commercial law to govern the case." The state decisions upon questions of commercial law would, therefore, "undoubtedly . . . receive the most deliberate attention and respect of this Court; but they cannot furnish positive rules, or conclusive authority, by which our own judgments are to be bound up and governed." Story added

Lord Mansfield's dictum that negotiable instruments were governed by the "general" commercial law, and then he concluded that section 34 did not provide the rule of decision in the *Swift* case.

> And we have not now the slightest difficulty in holding [the Justice said] that this section upon its true intendment and construction, is strictly limited to local statutes and local usages of the character before stated, and does not extend to contracts and other instruments of a commercial nature, the true interpretation and effect whereof are to be sought, not in the decisions of the local tribunals, but in the general principles and doctrines of commercial jurisprudence.[26]

Story devoted the bulk of his opinion to questions concerning the principle of negotiability raised in the case. He held first that creditors such as Swift possessed an absolute right of recovery against debtors in Tysen's position, irregardless of whether there was fraud involved in the original making of the bill giving rise to the debt. Story then extended this principle to commercial instruments drawn and received as "collateral" security for bona fide credit transactions. This point had been raised by neither the final argument nor the original record of the case. In this and his major point Story emphasized the extent to which a broad construction of the principle of negotiability was vital to commerce. "It is for the benefit and convenience of the commercial world," he exclaimed, "to give as wide an extent as practicable to the credit and circulation of negotiable paper." The security guaranteed by the commercial law, enabled the creditor, Story said, "to safely give a prolonged credit, or forebear from taking any legal steps to enforce his rights. The debtor also has the advantage of making his negotiable securities of equivalent value to cash." He estimated that "probably more than one half of all bank transactions in our country . . . are of this nature. The [contrary] doctrine would strike a fatal blow at all discounts of negotiable securities for preexisting debts."[27]

The Court gave unanimous assent to the decision; only

Justice Catron broke the silence with a concurring opinion. He quibbled with neither the resolution of the antecendent-debt question nor the interpretation given section 34. The Tennesseean disagreed only with the introduction of collateral securities into the decision. "I am unwilling to sanction the introduction into the opinion of this Court," he said, "a doctrine aside from the case made by the record, or argued by counsel . . . that a negotiable note or bill pledged as collateral security for a previous debt, is taken by the creditor in the due course of trade." A collateral security was a mere accommodation and, as such, rested on no real transaction of business. A holder of an accommodation should not, the justice continued, "stand on the foot of him who purchases in the market, or takes the instrument in extinguishment of a previous debt." Catron emphasized that state courts had refused to permit the defenses of the commercial law to collateral securities. It was "improbable," he said, "that they will yield to a mere expression of opinion of this Court . . . in conformity to the recent English cases referred to in the opinion." The acceptance of the principle would better wait until a case arose directly upon it in federal court. If the "question was permitted to rest until it fairly arose," the Justice said, "the decision of it either way by the Court, probably, would, and I think ought to settle it."[28]

THE MEANING OF SWIFT

The Supreme Court ordered the circuit court to reverse its instruction to the jury as to the rights governing Swift's bill of exchange. After nearly five years, Fessenden's plea that general commercial law should govern his client's rights finally won out. The decision itself went relatively unnoticed. Story used the case in his moot court at Harvard University where he was Dane Professor of Law. The arguments presented there, however, added nothing to those made during the case's several hearings. One newspaper stated that the decision "settled an important commercial question which ought to be soon generally known," while a law journal mentioned the case in similar terms. Nothing was said of the Court's interpretation of section 34. Given the notoriety of later years, this lack of attention concerning Story's opinion may seem surprising. Considering the decision in terms of the character of commercial jurisprudence and the role of the federal judiciary in enforcing that jurisprudence during the antebellum period, however, suggests a meaning quite different from that put forth by Brandeis, Holmes, and others.[29]

In several ways the *Swift* decision rested upon established assumptions concerning the federal courts' function in the federal system. The idea that federal tribunals represented an alternate choice to litigants seeking to avoid state courts was not new. Federal jurisdiction was restricted and limited: As one commentator noted in 1836, "Jurisdiction of federal courts is definite and specific and not general and it is therefore only in comparatively rare cases, that resort is had to them for redress of private wrongs." But for those engaged in interstate business, such limitations were of little concern. *Niles' Register* stated in 1825 that it was "almost a matter of course that a citizen of . . . [a] state, having a cause of any magnitude in amount of principle, steps over the line and becomes a temporary resident of another state, in order to avail himself of the jurisdiction of the United States Courts." These courts, noted *Hunt's Merchants' Magazine* in 1842 were those which "nonresidents are chiefly interested." Story in his *Commentaries on the Constitution* suggested further that a prime "tendency" of federal jurisdiction was "to increase the confidence and credit between the commercial and agricultural states. No man can be insensible to the value, in promoting credit, of the belief of there being a prompt, efficient, and impartial administration of justice in enforcing contracts."[30]

These views were not confined to nationalists like Story. Even extreme states' rights zealots like Abel Upshur (judge of the Virginia Supreme Court, publicist, U.S. secretary of state) conceded that sectional and state rivalry created the need for federal jurisdiction. Controversies "between citizens of different states," he said in 1836, "could not be entrusted to the tribunals of any particular state interested, or whose citizens are interested therein, without danger of injustice and partiality." Protection of interstate economic activity was, therefore, left to the federal judiciary. "Jurisdiction is given to the federal courts in these cases," Upshur continued, "simply because they are equally interested of all the parties, are the common courts of all parties, and are therefore presumed to form the only fair and impartial tribunal between them." The student of "discrepancies" in the nation's commercial law, William Wallace, extended Upshur's and Story's theme by suggesting that establishing uniformity in "the commercial common law . . . throughout the country" was possible "by giving, in all commercial cases . . . a right of direct appeal to the Supreme Court of the United States from the State Courts." Wallace acknowledged that establishing this right of appeal would require an alteration of the Constitution "which it would be difficult to obtain, but which, if obtained, would compensate the trouble."[31]

Why did Wallace, Upshur, and Story consider this forum shopping vital to American federalism? The legal confusion and uncertainty characteristic of the federal system increased the costs of doing business. A writer for the *North American Review* summed up the problems well in 1829. "The inconveniences arising from these diversities," he complained, "would seem . . . not only to trouble the lawyer and the courts, but to render the commercial and trading part of the community liable to perpetual mistakes, losses, and vexations." He then focused on the effect this fragmentation had on interstate commercial transactions of every sort. "As the means of internal communications with other states daily increases, a host of contracts, debts, liabilities, and transfers spring up. The means of securing debts, transferring real and personal property, and enforcing agreements in one state, become interesting to the inhabitants of other states who may transact business there."[32]

Outright local prejudice against out-of-state creditors was another source of uncertainty. Mercantile rivalry among the states and debtor influence on legislatures during hard times put pressure on local courts to favor in-state debtors over the nonresident creditors. Local juries also tended to distrust outsiders. Confusion in the local law of New York concerning the principle of negotiability was present in other states. Given the confused status of commercial law within the states and a marked rivalry among the states which threatened creditor rights, it was perhaps not surprising that contemporaries believed that the institution most capable of bringing order out of chaos was the federal judiciary. As a writer for the *North American Review* said as early as 1817: "The importance of uniform decisions in matters of common interest, and the real or supposed danger of partiality in the courts of the states, are well known to have been among the principal objects, for which the jurisdiction of the federal court was given."[33]

Uncertainty in the local law of the states was especially troubling where it undermined the uniformity of commercial jurisprudence. James Sullivan said in 1801 that "there ought to be one uniform rule throughout the nation on bills of exchange, promissory notes, insurance policies, and all personal contracts. These all arise from commerce, and the regulation of them is the regulation of commerce itself." It was "nonsense," he concluded, that a contract negotiable in one state was not negotiable in another. Little had changed by 1839 when Wallace bemoaned the considerable "discrepancies which exist among us in respect to our commercial law . . ." and, he continued, the "evil . . . is likely to increase rather than diminish." In his "Remarks upon Uniformity in Commercial Law," Wallace located the chief source of this confusion in the diffuse pattern of federal and state legal jurisdictions. The great "discrepancies" characterizing American commercial law were due, he asserted, "in a slight degree to . . . legislation, but principally . . . to the decisions of our state courts. Each state has its own courts and the decisions of one state are not binding on another." The United States, (in the federal judiciary) also "has its courts," he concluded, "but their decisions are not binding on the state courts, nor those of the state courts on them. Neither are the decisions of the Supreme Court of the United States binding on the state courts, except in very few cases."[34]

Besides the inability of the federal courts to control the mercantile decisions of the states, there were other sources of uncertainty in the nation's commercial law. Wallace's doctrinal "discrepancies" in part originated in the structure of the state judicial systems. One institutional source of uncertainty in the commercial law was the jury. During the eighteenth century, American juries had had considerable authority to determine both the law and facts governing a particular case. By the 1830s, judges had circumscribed this power through their instructions as to the law that should control the facts. Both systems, merchants complained, fostered confusion in the settlement of mercantile cases. Judges and laymen were ill-equipped to understand the intricacies of commercial transactions; judges, therefore, often applied the wrong law to a particular set of facts, while juries were unable to agree upon what the facts were. The problem manifested itself most frequently in the requirement that jurors agree unanimously on a verdict. "The frequent inability of jurors to agree in commercial cases . . . is a matter to be regretted," wrote a critic in *Hunt's*. "The ways of the law are slow and onerous enough. . . . We think there is great reason to suspect that in this system there has crept some foreign element, which thrives only upon the virtues it destroys, and is destructive of the very ends for which the system was designed."[35]

The spread of equity jurisdiction further undermined the uniformity of commercial jurisprudence. During the early nineteenth century, chancery courts came to exercise an ever growing influence in the local law of the states. This

growing influence was based on the chancellor's unique
powers: He could halt proceedings at law through injunc-
tions, collect evidence through bills of discovery, and even
rescind jury verdicts in the common law courts under certain circumstances. Because of these powers, and because
there were no juries in equity, mercantile interests increasingly brought commercial cases into chancery. As the chancellor's business increased, a rivalry developed with the
common-law courts in many states. A major outcome of this
rivalry (as we noted in the law court's misapplication of
Chancellor Kent's decision regarding preexisting debts in
New York) was confusion in the law regulating commercial
contracts. The legislature's occasional reorganization of
common law and equity jurisdictions contributed further to
legal uncertainty.[36]

Legislative interference in the judicial process could take
more extreme forms. From time to time, under pressure
from debtor interests, state legislatures seriously threatened
judicial independence. Legislatures sometimes went to the
extreme of closing the courts to prevent adjudication of
debtor-creditor disputes, made depreciated paper legal
tender for debts, allowed extensions of time to debtors
through stay laws (which were virtual moratoriums), and
even passed private acts to overturn court decisions. Often
these moves were motivated by efforts to protect in-state
debtors from out-of-state creditors. Massachusetts and New
York, commented Congressman Elijah H. Mills in 1818,
carried on a kind of "border war," in which each state used
its laws to favor locals at the expense of businessmen from
the neighboring state.[37]

During the distress of the Panic of 1819–1822, Kentucky,
Ohio, North Carolina, Indiana, Mississippi, Alabama, Tennessee, Maryland, and other states passed laws similar to
those in New York and Massachusetts in an effort to alle-
viate the burdens of state residents, many of whom were
indebted to creditors in other states. During the 1830s Alabama attempted to close her borders to corporations chartered in other states by passing a law which virtually denied

the validity of contracts negotiated between local entities and out-of-state corporations. But surely the most extreme example was Kentucky, a state which created a whole new judicial system to protect its debtors, while the old Kentucky judiciary continued to function at the same time, deciding cases in favor of in-state and out-of-state creditors.[38]

Merchants perceived the legal profession as another source of uncertainty in commercial cases. A writer for *Hunt's* noted that, "In this country, especially in our large cities, a large part of the legal business is of a commercial character. In these cities, the position of a sound commercial lawyer is enviable. It secures a lucrative practice and ultimate fame. We regard it, therefore, of the highest importance for an American lawyer to be acquainted with the . . . details of commerce . . . and . . . with all subjects of a mercantile character, as they are interwoven with the legal business of the country." Yet despite these rewards and the need for legal certainty, the article complained, "many ludicrous mistakes have occurred by reason of the ignorance of judges and lawyers upon . . . commercial subjects."[39]

Behind these institutional factors lay a general ambiguity in contemporaries' views of the sources of commercial law. Although few nineteenth-century lawyers would have doubted that commercial law was ultimately man-made and hence capable of being changed for the purpose of promoting desired social policies, some courts and commercial lawyers placed a heavy emphasis upon precedent and legal stability. The Massachusetts Supreme Judicial Court, for example, would follow precedent explicitly in any case where the law "must be considered as settled" by a prior decision and it was, as a result "probable that . . . mercantile contracts have been generally entered into with a view to that law. . . ." A further reason for following judge-made rules, according to a writer in *Hunt's,* was that precedent was often "grounded upon principles of universal equity." Judges, it was urged, should "consult precedents established by their predecessors . . . extract from those precedents . . . ethical principles . . . and clearly . . .

point them out in . . . opinions." There was "nothing more surprising," the writer for *Hunt's* continued, than the "admirable coincidence" existing between "ancient and modern judicial precedents . . . extending from . . . ancient Rome to . . . modern America constituting a uniform and perfect system of practical ethics."[40]

An alternative conception gave little weight to precedent, emphasizing instead that the "flexibility of the common law is a quality of vast importance to . . . a young and improved nation." Commercial law was, said another writer for *Hunt's*, the "newest branch" of the common law, and "as a system in daily application, has grown, and is growing, out of the wants and habits of this commercial age." Merchants themselves, concluded the commentator, contributed "to the system of mercantile law . . . [whose] great principles . . . elaborated by the learning and genius of judges . . . were after all, but gems, snatched in the rough by the moilers of the law from the rushing stream of daily commerce."[41]

All this undermined the importance of precedent in American commercial law. James Kent's *Commentaries on American Law* pointed this out. "I wish not to . . . press too strongly the doctrine of *stare decisis,* when I recollect there are more than one thousand cases to be pointed out in the English and American books of reports, which have been overruled, doubted, or limited in their application." Given these considerations, Kent urged the value of wise experimentalism in judicial decision making. "It is probable that the records of many courts in this country are replete with hasty and crude decisions," he said; "such cases ought to be examined without fear, and revised without reluctance, rather than to have the character of our laws impaired, and the beauty and harmony of the system destroyed by perpetuity of error. Even a series of decisions are not always conclusive evidence of what is law," the judge concluded; "the revision of a decision very often resolves itself into a mere question of expediency." Behind Kent's suspicion of reliance on precedent was perhaps a general conviction that law must be flexible to adapt to the constant change so characteristic of antebellum America. Many Americans of the period held the view that in law, as in "every branch of human inquiry . . . the veneration of authority has been one of the principle barriers to human improvement."[42]

Antebellum lawyers and judges were never able to determine exactly which conception should govern their application of general commercial principles. This failure left the status of commercial jurisprudence in the local law of the states shrouded in "numerous legal doubts," said David Hoffman (law professor of the University of Maryland and author of the influential *A Course of Legal Study*). Uncertainty over whether precedent or mercantile practice was the best guide in the resolution of commercial disputes, meant that the question was left to the independent judgment of the judges themselves. "So long as the struggle between precedent and reason shall continue," noted the *North American Review,* "legal opinions . . . will depend more on the character and turn of mind of the judge, who is to decide it, than any general principle."[43]

Ironically, then, American judges were at once the source of and solution for pervasive uncertainty in the commercial jurisprudence of the local law of the states. The federal judiciary and the courts of the states operated, as Wallace pointed out, separately and independently of one another insofar as the adjudication of commercial disputes was concerned. State and federal judges exercised an independent judgment as to the proper rule of decision in mercantile cases; and it was left to these judges to determine for themselves sound principles of commercial law. Many factors involving the character of the state judiciaries often impeded the formulation of uniform rules in local jurisdictions, as the example of New York showed. This was less true in the federal courts, for reasons that will become apparent. But whether a mercantile case arose in state or federal court, judges faced the perplexing problem that they lacked a legal theory with which to establish uniform commercial principle throughout the federal system.

These were the elements of jurisprudence underpinning the *Swift* decision. The recognized value of "forum shopping" in a federal system fraught with uncertainty, the acknowledged prerogative of state and federal judges to determine for themselves rules of decision in commercial cases without regard to each others' authority, and the preference for a "wise experimentalism" over *stare decisis* were fundamentals of the antebellum legal order. Behind these fundamentals was a marked ambiguity in the conception of the nature and source of law. This ambiguity created the need for a legal theory that might facilitate uniformity in commercial jurisprudence. It was widely assumed that general principles of commercial law (like the principles of Newtonian physics) could be determined and applied in mercantile cases. The difficulty arose, however, in ascertaining whether commercial practice or judicial precedent was the surest guide to what constituted general principles. Story's extensive discussion of banking and mercantile practice suggested that the court found commercial usage to be the better guide in *Swift* v. *Tyson*.

However, identifying the jurisprudential elements underlying *Swift* gives only a partial explanation of the decision. Besides the idea of general law, the opinion held that federal courts were bound to follow state law in cases involving local issues. The distinction between general and local law was one that was worked out gradually from the 1790s to 1842 in the federal courts. Tracing the evolution of this distinction will contribute further to an understanding of the meaning of Story's opinion. It will also—when considered in conjunction with the general jurisprudential themes— provide a more complete basis for explaining the unanimity of the Court and the reasons why Jacksonian judges could readily distinguish certain commercial issues from the sensitive question of federal jurisdiction over the common law.

St. George Tucker in his commentaries on Blackstone in 1803 stated the Jeffersonian view toward a federal common law. "For, if it be true that the common law of England has been adopted by the United States in their national, or federal capacity, the jurisdiction of the *federal courts* must be coextensive with it; or, in other words, *unlimited.*" After much resistance, the Court finally accepted Tucker's analysis insofar as it applied to the criminal law in *United States* v. *Coolidge* in 1816.

In other cases the Court also refused to uphold a broad common-law jurisdiction. The celebrated case of *Wheaton* v. *Peters* (1834) demonstrated how far federal judges could go in this direction. This famous case involved a disputed copyright to published volumes of the *United States Reports.* During the early nineteenth century, copyright law was obscure and uncertain in America and was not absolutely settled in England. There was little agreement over whether the common law could protect copyright in the absence of a clear statutory provision. Even though the law was confused, Henry Wheaton argued that his right was guaranteed by the common law. A divided Supreme Court speaking through John McLean flatly rejected Wheaton's claim in sweeping terms. "The federal government is composed of twenty-four sovereign and independent states; each of which may have its local usages, customs, and common law." There is no principle, he said, "which pervades the union and has the authority of law, that is not embodied in the constitution or laws of the union. The common law could be made a part of our federal system only by legislative adoption."[44]

In dissent Smith Thompson and Henry Baldwin refused to accept McLean's argument. "I do not perceive," Thompson said, "how it becomes necessary in this case to decide the question whether we have here any code of laws known and regarded as the common law of the United States." The case involved a right of property, the justice said, "and in such cases the state laws form the rules of decision in the courts of the United States; and the case now before the court must be governed by the law of . . . the state of Pennsylvania [the state in which the case arose]." Thompson then went on to show that after the Revolution, the legislature passed a reception statute recognizing the common law as the basis of Pennsylvania's law (subject only to local alterations and adoptions). Thus, even though no state law existed specifically on copyright, federal judges could apply the English common-law rule because implicitly it had been made part of the local law by the reception statute. This view was elaborated in more detail in Baldwin's *General View of the Constitution*. The dissenters' position in the *Wheaton* case set forth one theory, shared by other writers of treatises during the period, which recognized a limited scope for independent judgment in settling common-law disputes coming into federal court.[45]

Thompson's dissent suggests that, despite McLean's strong opinion to the contrary, there was room for federal judicial discretion in determining cases at common law. A determination of the scope of this discretion will help us understand how contemporaries viewed the command in section 34 that "the laws of the several states . . . shall be regarded as rules of decision in trials at common law in the courts of the United States in cases where they apply." Crucial to an understanding of this phrase will be the meaning of the word *laws* and a consideration of those cases in which these laws were to "apply" as rules of decision. Even though acknowledging a limited discretionary power, Thompson's dissent recognized the most important instance in which courts applied local law as the rule of decision: in those cases involving rights to property.

An early example of how federal courts deferred to local custom in property cases, even at the expense of the national government, was *United States* v. *Crosby* (1812). In this case the federal government claimed some Massachusetts land in possession of one Jonah Crosby. In the circuit court, Story instructed the jury according to state customs favoring Crosby's claim to the land, and the jury's verdict went his way. The government appealed to the circuit court, where Story again upheld the defendant. The government then appealed the case to the Supreme Court. There, a unanimous Court finally settled the matter in Crosby's favor. Speaking for the Court, Story said that the purpose of the Massachusetts local custom was to ensure the uniformity of rights in private land transactions through maintaining the role of the registry system. There was "no doubt on the subject," the justice concluded, and the Court was "clearly of the opinion that the title to the land can be acquired and lost only in the manner prescribed by the law of the place where such land is situated." In *Jackson* v. *Chew* Thompson followed this reasoning where there was a long line of state court precedents establishing a settled rule governing real property. And in *Green* v. *Neal* in 1832 McLean held that federal judges would defer to state statutes controlling certain questions of property rights.[46]

These decisions suggest that federal judges considered themselves bound by the local law in cases involving real estate and other property matters. As we have seen, they also refused to exercise an independent judgment where common-law crimes, common-law copyright, and jurisdiction based on a common-law right were at issue. There were other cases, however, in which the federal courts did not follow the local law. A striking example of how even staunch Jeffersonians asserted a discretionary independence over rules of decision, ignoring state law, was *Daley's Lessee* v. *James* (1823). In this case, which involved an issue precisely the same as that in *Jackson* v. *Chew*, William Johnson refused to make a state supreme court opinion the rule of decision; he did so, he said, because only two of the three state judges agreed on the decision.[47]

Where equity or common-law process was the issue, the federal judiciary took even a stronger stand against state law. In *Robinson* v. *Campbell* (1818) the question arose whether Tennessee statutes could prevent federal judges from applying equity remedies or common-law procedures, which in effect blunted the operation of the state law. The argument was put forth that section 34 of the Judiciary Act of 1789 made the Tennessee statutes the rule of decision in federal court. To this claim Justice Thomas Todd, in a unanimous decision, held that (because early acts of Congress granted such in vague terms) "remedies in the courts

of the United States are to be at common law or in equity,
not according to the practice of state courts, but according
to the principles of common law and equity, as distinguished and defined in . . . [England]." Kent in his *Commentaries* said that the opinion "went far towards the admission of the existence and application of the common law to
civil cases in the federal courts." In a forceful decision regarding the operation of Kentucky statutes under section
34 in 1825, Marshall also upheld the obligation of federal
judges to ignore state laws if they interfered with federal
judicial process. In numerous circuit court decisions, this
principle was repeatedly upheld.[48]

From the 1790s on, federal courts also applied an independent judgment on a wide scale in litigation involving
commercial law. During the first decade of the federal judiciary's existence, federal judges showed a clear but poorly
defined willingness to make commercial principles the rule
of decision in mercantile cases. In several suits involving
foreign and domestic merchants, federal judges freely borrowed those principles of commercial jurisprudence integrated into the common law by Mansfield. They did the
same in litigation where the first Bank of the United States
was a party. In cases expressly dealing with section 34, however, the Supreme Court appeared unable to formulate a
definite rule governing jurisdiction over commercial law.
This was apparent in *Brown* v. *Van Braam* in 1797. A Rhode
Island statute and the state's local common law were unclear
as to the rights of parties to a bill of exchange. Although
counsel for both the litigants agreed that the matter should
be settled according to commercial principles, they disputed
the extent to which federal courts could apply these principles without some provision for receiving them into the local law. After some discussion the Supreme Court decided
in favor of the creditor by holding that the "law merchant"
had been received into the local law of Rhode Island under
the state's reception statute. Thus, under section 34, the law
merchant provided the rule decision through the local law,

even in the absence of any showing as to what the local law was in fact.[49]

Comments by Justice Samuel Chase suggested the Court's uncertainty in the matter. The reporter showed that Chase concurred in the opinion of the Court but that it was on common law principles and not in compliance with the laws and practice of the state. "I shall be governed, in forming my opinion," the justice concluded emphatically, "by what the common law says must be the effect of a judgment . . . without regarding the practice of the State." If, "indeed," Chase stressed, "the practice of the several states were, in every case, to be adopted, we should be involved in an endless labyrinth of false constructions, and idle forms."[50]

During the tenure of Chief Justice John Marshall, the Court showed a strong inclination to apply principles of commercial law but refused to establish a general theory for doing so. In two cases in 1801 and 1802, the federal circuit court upheld the commercial law, ignoring a Virginia statute. In an appeal in one of the cases, *Mandeville* v. *Riddle,* Marshall overruled the lower court and made the state law the rule of decision, but six years later when the case was appealed again, this time in equity, Marshall followed the mercantile rule. In cases where no state statute was involved, Marshall was more direct in applying commercial principles. In *Coolidge* v. *Payson* (1817), the rights as to a bill received in payment of a preexisting debt were disputed. The circuit court followed the commercial law; the case was then appealed to the Supreme Court. "It is of much importance to merchants," Marshall said, "that this question be at rest." After a lengthy discussion of both local and international law on the subject, Marshall upheld the circuit court.[51]

In other cases heard before 1835, federal judges developed what amounted to a federal commercial jurisprudence, though they did so without facing squarely section 34. Marshall, perhaps because of states' rights scrutiny and criticism of the federal judiciary, received mercantile rules obliquely into the corpus of federal law. Nothing revealed this more clearly than the case of *Van Reimsdyk* v. *Kane* in 1812. Again a Rhode Island statute governing a foreign debt contracted through a bill of exchange was in question. In denying the reach of the statute, Story went farther than any other federal judge of the period in formulating a comprehensive theory of the status of commercial jurisprudence under section 34. "I hold it to be a legitimate inference," the judge said, "that a contract made in a foreign country or state . . . cannot be discharged by a mere positive regulation of another country or state." Story agreed that federal courts followed section 34 where applicable, but there "must . . . be some limitation" to the "operation of this clause, and I apprehend such a limitation must arise whenever the subject matter is extra-territorial."[52]

The national courts were established in order to protect the rights of citizens of different states and nations from unfavorable local law. In "controversies affecting citizens of other states . . . as for instance, foreign contracts of a commercial nature, I think it can hardly be maintained, that the laws of a state . . . are to be the exclusive guides for judicial decision." Following this reasoning, Story construed section 34. "I should have little hesitation," he said, "in affirming that a discharge under the insolvent law of Rhode Island was not a discharge of the contract in the present suit; and that it is not a case, in which the law of the state is to be exclusively regarded, as the rule of decision." Story concluded with a graphic description of potential catastrophic consequences if local law bound federal courts in all commercial matters under section 34. "It would enable the state legislatures by local regulations, to dry up the sources of the federal jurisdiction, and annihilate public as well as private credit; it would," said Story, "set the citizens of the different states in array against each other, and enable a fraudulent debtor to retreat into another state, and there by a formal surrender of his property and a settled residence, to set at defiance the claims of all his absent and honest creditors."[53]

Marshall's treatment of Story's *Van Reimsdyk* decision suggests how unwilling he was to formulate a broad theory to interpret section 34. When the case reached the Supreme Court on appeal in *Clark's Executors* v. *Van Reimsdyk* (1815), Marshall accepted Story's reasoning to a point. He agreed that the commercial law should govern contracts made between citizens of different states and nations. But Marshall refused even to discuss Story's construction of section 34. The case was sent back to the circuit court in order to ascertain more precisely the status of the commercial law on the subject in Batavia, the place where the contract was originally drawn. Marshall's refusal to recognize Story's construction of section 34 suggests his caution in ignoring the local statutes of the states. As *Coolidge* and other cases showed, he did not hesitate to borrow commercial principles from the common law where no statute was at issue; but Marshall refused to formulate any doctrine upon which to base this indirect reception of common-law rules. Perhaps this hesitancy was due to popular resistance to anything suggesting a federal common law. Throughout Marshall's tenure, federal jurisdiction was under sporadic but persistent attack from states' rights advocates. Whatever the reason for Marshall's caution, it was evident that Story's theory was not accepted by the Supreme Court until Taney's chief justiceship.[54]

After Marshall's death in 1835, Story applied his ideas in several circuit court decisions. He stated his view precisely in 1838. In matters involving "general principles of the commercial law, federal courts possess the general authority, which belongs to the state tribunals, and are not bound by the local decisions." This did not mean state law was ignored but that it was not binding. Federal judges, he continued, "are at liberty to consult their own opinions, guided indeed, by the greatest deference for the knowledge, learning, and ability of the state tribunals, but still exercising their own judgment, as to reasons, on which those decisions are founded."[55]

In 1841, Justice McLean on circuit was receptive to

Story's views. *Riley* v. *Anderson* arose in Ohio and involved facts and issues very similar to those in the *Swift* case. The state supreme court had applied New York precedents denying recovery on a bill of exchange. McLean reviewed these decisions, noted that they were unsettled, cited English cases upholding the commercial law principle and pointed out that the United States Supreme Court had twice followed the English rule. Against these authorities, should the federal court follow the Ohio opinion as the rule of decision? The justice referred to the instances in which the national tribunals adhered to the local law. "The construction of a statute by the supreme court of a state is followed by this court," McLean conceded, "as it constitutes a rule of property and as the rule should be the same in the courts of the United States." But this same uniformity was indispensable to the predictability of commercial transactions, "and for the same reason on all questions of a general and commercial character, the rule established by the federal courts should be followed by the local tribunals." Thus, he concluded, since the "question is not local but of a general interest, the decision in Ohio does not constitute the rule for this court." The rule governing the case, therefore, "must be considered as resting on general principles."[56]

McLean's decision suggests that Story's views on section 34 were gaining a wider hearing after Marshall's passing. These views were not, however, original to Justice Joseph Story, even in the years before 1835. After 1800 a number of commentators put forth a similar interpretation of section 34 with regards to the commercial law. In 1801 in his *History of Land Titles,* James Sullivan stated that contract cases in federal courts, because they "arose from commerce; . . . ought to be governed by the *jus gentium,* the law of nations, known and established over the commercial world." The respectable Jeffersonian St. George Tucker held virtually the same opinion in 1803: "the law of nations, the common law of England . . . the law merchant . . . must in their turn be resorted to as the rule of decision in federal tribunals, according to the nature and circumstances of each case, respectively. So that each of these laws may be regarded, so far as they apply to such cases, respectively, as the law of the land." In 1824, Peter DuPonceau argued in an essay on federal jurisdiction that federal judges were free to consult the "general law received by all the commercial world" in deciding commercial cases; William Rawle's *View of the Constitution* in 1829 took the same position, as did Thomas Sergeant's respected *Constitutional Law* in 1830.[57]

Federal court decisions and several legal treatises suggest how federal judges interpreted section 34 during the half century before the *Swift* case came to the Supreme Court. There seems little room for doubt that the "laws of the several states" included statutes, decisions by state courts, and vaguely defined "local customs"; it also seems fairly certain that federal judges asserted a limited discretionary authority to determine what were the cases in which the local law should be "applied" as the rule of decision. By the 1830s it was clear that federal judges were bound by state law in cases involving rights to real property and in several other minor or politically sensitive kinds of disputes such as common-law crimes. At the same time it was apparent that in equity, process, and commercial cases, federal courts did not consider themselves obligated to follow the state law. The authority to apply an independent judgment in equity and process litigation was based on vague provisions of federal laws, but no such ground existed in commercial cases. Marshall resisted the formulation of an express theory governing federal jurisdiction over the commercial law, even though he freely resorted to it many times. Thus the *Swift* case provided the Supreme Court of Chief Justice Taney an opportunity for judicial policy making in an area where policy was both needed and unclear. The circuit decisions of Story and McLean suggested the form and substance such a policy might take.

Noting the extent to which Story's opinion was rooted in the legal order that had evolved by 1840 provides a reasonable (though admittedly speculative) explanation for the perplexing unanimity of the *Swift* decision. The justice's construction of section 34 rested upon a distinction between general and local law which was familiar to antebellum lawyers and judges. Thus, placing commercial jurisprudence outside the reach of section 34 did not of itself challenge the states' rights values of Daniel, Taney, and others. The fact that the case did not involve a state statute or the rights of a corporation further removed the issue from the shadow of state sovereignty. On circuit, in cases involving debtor-creditor issues similar to those present in *Swift,* Daniel had upheld creditor rights. The Virginian's famous proclivity for dissent always involved corporations or particular federal power, such as admiralty jurisdiction. An independent judgment in cases involving interstate mercantile transactions was consistent with views concerning federal jurisdiction held by Upshur, Tucker, Justice Johnson, and other states' rights supporters.[58]

Prior to 1835, especially during Chief Justice Marshall's tenure, the Court declined to interpret section 34. In each case where the opportunity to do so arose, however, a state statute rather than confused state precedents, was at issue. In other cases, the Court applied commercial principles without comment (as in *Coolidge* v. *Payson*) or relied upon a strained interpretation of federal process acts (as in *Wayman* v. *Southard*). Marshall's strategy in commercial litigation involving state statutes was exemplified in the *Van Reimsdyk* case. He upheld the creditor's rights in equity, while refusing to confront the meaning of section 34 as Story had urged on circuit. But the chief justice's cautious approach seemed unsatisfactory as suits arising out of interstate transactions increased by the 1830s. The circuit opinions of McLean and Story evidenced the mounting need for action by the Supreme Court. Writers of legal treatises—including Sullivan, DuPonceau, Rawles, and Sergeant—had established the basis for such action years before.

These considerations suggest the conclusion that the central question in *Swift* v. *Tyson* involved commercial law rather than federal-state relations. Justice Catron's concurring opinion offers further evidence for this view. Catron did not mention section 34 and agreed with Story's opinion concerning the principle of negotiability. The Tennessee Democrat disputed only the introduction into the opinion of a rule that had been raised neither by the record of the case nor the argument of counsel. This rule extended the principle of negotiability to commercial paper drawn or held as collateral security for debts. In criticizing this result of the *Swift* decision, Catron voiced concerns put forth by others during the period. But the criticism involved essentially a rather technical point; it did not represent a philosophical position grounded on states' rights.[59]

More than anything else, however, the nature of American legal thought explained the meaning of *Swift* and the court's unanimity in deciding it. In the minds of antebellum lawyers and judges, the idea of a general commercial law was held independent of and separate from notions of state sovereignty or jurisdictional authority. All courts, state and federal, possessed the power to apply mercantile principles in commercial cases. This power rested upon the assumption that mercantile principles governed commercial activity, and that man-made mercantile rules should be as nearly as possible in harmony with these principles. Story's statement that the New York cases were not "laws" but merely evidence of universal principles of human conduct was consistent with this widely held assumption. The justice's argument failed, however, to state the extent to which the notion of the "general law" was shrouded in ambiguity. While there was consensus as to the existence of general principles, there was little agreement on how judges and lawyers might ascertain and apply these principles in real cases. Confusion on this point was evidenced by the inability of writers for *Hunt's* and *North American Review* to state precisely whether precedent or mercantile usage was the surest guide to what constituted general commercial principles in American courts.

It is possible, therefore, to view the *Swift* decision as an effort to give federal judges a theoretical justification for recourse to international jurisprudence in adjudication of commercial cases. The *Swift* decision established expressly a rule governing federal judges' choice of law. In determining commercial principles, federal courts were not to confine themselves to the precedents of any local jurisdiction, but should scan the entire landscape of American, English, and civil law. As to the standards upon which judges should base their choice of principle, Story said that business necessity and usage were the best guides (as shown by his extensive discussion of the practical significance of negotiability in antebellum banking and mercantile practice).

According to this reading, Story's opinion represented an effort to provide federal judges with what amounted to a theory of conflict of laws. In the *Van Reimsdyk* case of 1812 he had unsuccessfully tried to do the same thing by holding that "extraterritorial" issues were not to be governed by section 34. More than 30 years later, Story elaborated in more detail virtually the same idea in his *Commentaries on Conflict of Laws*. In this book, which became the classic treatment of the subject in the nineteenth century, Story pointed out that it was not yet clear whether local law or principles of international jurisprudence should control commercial contracts. The traditional rule was that contracts were governed by the law of the place where they were made, but that in "civil commerce" exceptions arose, which were regulated by a "wise and liberal regard for common convenience and mutual necessities." In the "complicated" federal system of the United States, as well as the rest of the world, the lack of "international principles in matters of private right" threatened "intolerable grievances," to "weaken all domestic relations," and to "destroy the sanctity of contracts and the security of property."[60]

The justice admitted that the sovereign state had ultimate authority to determine what law could be applied within its borders. At the same time, however, a "final judge" was necessary to determine those exceptions in which "public convenience" called for the administration of "extraterritorial" principles. In "England and America," Story exclaimed, "the Courts through the common law, have met . . . the

exigencies of the times . . . and so far as the practice of
nations . . . has been supposed to furnish any general principle, it has been followed . . . with a wise and manly lib-
erality." The standards that should guide judicial discretion
in choosing "general principles," were "mutual interest and
utility . . . and a sense of moral necessity to do justice in
order that justice may be done to us in return." In such
cases, courts "presume the tacit adoption" of general rules
derived from international mercantile practice based on
"comity." This was "not the comity of the courts, but the
comity of the nation which is administered and ascertained
in the same way and guided by the same reasoning, by
which all other principles of municipal law are ascertained
and guided."[61]

Whether the Court actually intended that the concept of
general law should function as a theory of conflicts is, of
course, disputable. But given the uncertainty of the nation's
local law, and the unique role of the federal courts in ame-
liorating this uncertainty, when federal judges decided cases
according to the general law their logical process would re-
semble that described by Story as "comity." In a mercantile
dispute the judge must consider principles that composed
the jurisprudential amalgam known as international private
law. His authority for doing so would be based on the right
of discretionary judgment lodged, as Wallace said, in all
courts when deciding commercial cases. The criterion for
the selection of the appropriate principle (as it was in *Swift*)
must be "utility," as defined by the necessities of mercantile
practice and the standards of jurisprudential reasoning.
The fact that the Court's opinion in the *Alabama Bank Cases*
in 1839 cited Story's *Commentaries on Conflict of Laws* shows
that the justices deciding *Swift* were familiar with the concept of comity. Certainly the language of *Swift*, the line of
reasoning in Story's treatise, the justice's other writings on
commercial law, and the conception of law presented in
Hunt's and the *North American Review* agree on this point.[62]

Whatever relationship there may have been in the minds
of the justices between the concept of general commercial

law and that of comity, it seems certain that *Swift* gave federal judges a theoretical foundation for applying discretionary judgment in commercial cases, where no such theory
had existed before. And the formalization of this discretionary power had implications beyond the level of legal theory.
Swift established a rule governing the entire federal judiciary, implemented through the Supreme Court's review of
jury instructions and the appellate process generally. Using
Swift as their guide, the federal judiciary—the only judicial
system whose authority reached throughout the entire
union—possessed a rule which made possible the formulation of a federal commercial law, governing all those who
came within its jurisdiction. Of course, as Wallace, Upshur,
and Story said, no one imagined that federal judges possessed authority over state courts, any more than state
judges had the power to instruct their brothers on the federal bench. Thus, the commercial law of the federal and
state courts might evolve separately of one another. But it
also suggested that a central assuption underlying *Swift* was
that state courts were expected to exercise their own discretion in formulating commercial jurisprudence. This meant
that Story's opinion recognized the authority (however
much the justice himself may have bemoaned the actual results) of state judges to develop a commercial law on their
own.

The result of the 1842 decision was to confirm the role of
the federal courts as alternative tribunals to those of the
states. This served the interests of merchants involved in
interstate trade, but it was consistent with the purposes defended by Upshur and others. Diversity jurisdiction gave
these merchants access to federal courts, which removed
them from the uncertainty and erratic prejudice of the local
law of the states. Once in the federal forum, merchants had
the opportunity to argue that their case should be governed
by the principles of the commercial law. The *Swift* doctrine
encouraged the lower federal court judges to apply these
principles, subject to appeal to the circuits and to the Supreme Court. The link between federal jurisdiction and

commercial principles aided the stability of the credit system and reduced the costs of interstate mercantile transactions. In performing this function, federal courts also helped support the influence of merchants in the national economy. This support may have, as Story said in 1833, reduced tensions between commercial and agricultural interests. The fact that states' rights proponents sanctioned such a role suggests perhaps that Story was right. At the same time, however, the federal judiciary's willingness to uphold commercial principles displayed an indirect preference for values which could favor not only creditors' rights, but sharp practices and opportunistic schemes (as the facts of the *Swift* case clearly show).[63]

These considerations suggest useful perspective on the "problem" of *Swift*. It seems apparent—Justice Brandeis and *Erie* to the contrary not withstanding—that federal-state relations were implicit and probably only secondary factors in the case. In getting beyond the traditional view, Horwitz and Dickinson offer valuable insight. Emphasis on the importance of commercial rules in the development of national commerce and evidence that the case involved primarily the application of a contemporary conception of commercial jurisprudence are essential to an understanding of the decision. Yet neither of these contributions addresses the hard question of why Taney's Jacksonian majority did what Marshall refused to do. Failure to address this problem leads to further difficulties. The contention that *Swift* represented an effort to force developmental mercantile rules upon unwilling state courts cannot be reconciled with the fact that Daniel and other states' rights supporters concurred in the opinion.

Dickinson's argument actually goes far to explain the Court's unanimity. By holding (as did Wallace, Upshur, and other antebellum commentators) that any judge—whether state or federal—was free to determine for himself appropriate principles of commercial law, Dickinson gets around the question of unanimity. Daniel and Story agreed, according to Dickinson's view, because they shared with their con-

temporaries a particular conception of commercial jurisprudence grounded in the behavior of the mercantile
world. But if this is true, how to account for the disparity
between the actions of the Marshall and Taney courts? If a
shared premise of jurisprudential thinking explains *Swift,*
then Marshall should have applied the premise in construing section 34. He had the opportunity to do so in the *Van
Reimsdyk* case. The chief justice's refusal to confront
squarely the meaning of section 34 in this case suggests that
more was involved in the problem of *Swift* than Dickinson
thought.

Consideration of several interrelated developments that
culminated in 1842 leads to another evaluation of Story's
opinion. Contemporaries' acceptance of the need for forum
shopping and the recognized independent authority of state
and federal judges over commercial law were norms em-
bodies in both Marshall's opinions and the *Swift* decision.
The main difference between the two involved state statutes.
Where a state statute was at issue, Marshall resorted to
strained applications of federal process acts to defeat state
authority (as he did in *Van Reimsdyk*). This approach, while
politically astute, did not offer a clear guide in resolving
commercial questions. By 1840 the growth of interstate
credit transactions and the dislocation created by the
depression pointed toward the need to formulate a clear
policy. As Dana stated in his argument before the Supreme
Court, the question raised in *Swift* "is now presented in a
form that calls for a specific and final decision of the whole
matter."[64] While Dana's comment dealt primarily with controversy surrounding section 34, his emphasis on the
"form" of the issue seems noteworthy. The Court was presented (apparently for the first time) with a case that did
not involve a state statute; it did, however, raise the question whether commercial law was within the meaning of section 34.

This combination of external events and the particular
character of the case may explain the Court's willingness to
do what Dana urged. Once given the opportunity denied

Marshall, states' rights supporters could view the problem solely in terms of jurisprudential assumptions that did not involve state sovereignty. Story carefully crafted his opinion within the limits of these assumptions, thus providing the basis for unanimity. Cotton planters such as Daniel, as much as commercially oriented justices like Story, understood the importance of uniform commercial rules to the smooth operation of the antebellum credit system. Presented with a case that embodied no direct federal-state issue, the justices were free to decide the commercial questions accordingly.[65]

The *Swift* case, then, may be understood as an attempt to balance federal jurisdiction over commercial jurisprudence with the need to respect the authority of local law. In achieving this balance, however, potential irony lurked. Story's opinion glossed over the extent to which the theoretical underpinnings of the idea of general commercial law were shrouded in ambiguity. By suggesting that business practice was the best guide in determining the principles of mercantile behavior, the justice ignored the equally valid arguments of commentators who favored precedent. Given the relative lack of concern for *stare decisis* noted by Kent and others, Story's approach was perhaps understandable. But this reliance upon practice and utility over precedent was in many ways the most significant part of the decision. Relying upon utilitarian considerations federal judges could now enlarge the reach of their authority on a scale that would have been much more difficult if Marshall's approach to commercial litigation had remained in force. Such an extension of federal judicial power—in marked contrast with the narrow terms of Story's opinion—could not help but threaten state authority. In the years after 1842 this possibility became reality. A decision that involved federal-state relations only on a secondary level would be applied so as to profoundly shape the future character of American federalism.

Chapter II

Swift Transformed

Swift *v.* Tyson *became a headless monster, marked down for destruction by all right thinking men.*

Grant Gilmore, *The Ages of American Law*

Between 1842 and the end of the nineteenth century the *Swift* doctrine underwent a gradual but fundamental transformation. It involved the Supreme Court's development of a theory that based the federal judiciary's discretionary authority over local law on the Constitution itself. Applying this theory, federal judges fashioned a true federal common law that went beyond the narrow terms set down in Story's opinion. After the Civil War the Court's action became the focus of heated debate that divided the nation's bar and raised challenging questions concerning the proper limits of federal judicial power in the federal system.

THE DOCTRINE BECOMES PART OF THE CONSTITUTION

The attack upon the *Swift* doctrine that emerged in the late nineteenth century, and the theory of federalism that grew out of this critical assault, held that the 1842 decision violated fundamental tenets of American constitutionalism. An evaluation of this contention depends upon an un-

45

derstanding of how the *Swift* doctrine came to be identified
with the enforcement of the grant of judicial authority
given in Article III of the Constitution. In order to establish
a basis for understanding how and why this "constitution-
alization" of *Swift* occurred, careful attention to the development of case law from 1842 to the 1890s seems appropriate. Analysis of this litigation in the context of the
changing federal system should suggest what factors contributed to the transformation of the doctrine; it will also
lay the foundation for the argument that the critics were
more influenced by immediate social and political considerations than an accurate understanding of the historical evolution of the *Swift* principle.

During the same term in which the Court decided *Swift,*
it handed down *Carpenter* v. *The Providence Washington Insurance Co.* This unanimous opinion written by Justice Story
followed the same reasoning as the earlier decision, while
extending the "general law" to include insurance contracts.[1]
In the same year, the Ohio Supreme Court reversed an earlier decision regarding the negotiability of commercial paper in order to follow the principle established in *Swift.* The
Ohio court held that "the law, as thus settled by the highest
judicial tribunal in the country will become the uniform
rule of all as it is now of most of the states." This was sound
commercial policy, the court concluded, because "in a country like ours, where so much communication and inter-
change exist between the different members of the confed-
eracy, to preserve uniformity in the great principles of
commercial law, is of much interest to the mercantile
world."[2] By 1849 state supreme courts in Alabama, Michigan, North Carolina, and New Jersey had accepted Story's
opinion at least in so far as it applied to certain forms of
negotiable paper. Only the New York high court flatly denied the validity of *Swift* in *Stalker* v. *McDonald.* Ironically,
James Kent disapproved of this case, arguing that he considered Story's decision as establishing the "plainer and better doctrine."[3]

By the 1850s *Swift* v. *Tyson* had acquired the status of a "leading case" in matters of commercial law. J. I. C. Hare and H. B. Wallace stated this in various editions of their *American Leading Cases.* Theophilus Parsons, professor of commercial law at Harvard, repeated the same view in several works. These commentators did not discuss Story's construction of section 34, though Parsons did suggest that he accepted the basic notion of the general law. *Hunt's Merchants' Magazine* in 1847 presented a similar view in a review of "Leading Cases Upon Commercial Law." John William Wallace discussed the character of commercial law in the United States in an address given before the University of Pennsylvania Law School, noting the rule of *Swift* as it applied to commercial paper. This presentation was an enlarged version of an earlier article published in 1836; it repeated the same points, including the view that the remedy for the confused state of local mercantile jurisprudence in the states was a direct review by the United States Supreme Court in all such cases. Giving the Court this authority would establish in the United States, Wallace concluded, the "truth of Lord Mansfield's declaration, that the Law Merchant is part of the Law of Nations—the Public Law of the Civilized world."[4]

These comments suggest a general acquiescence in the principle and theory established in the *Swift* decision, lasting through the decade before the Civil War. During the same period, the Supreme Court began enlarging the original scope of the doctrine (though this process met repeated dissent). In 1845 the federal judiciary's obligation to follow a Mississippi Supreme Court's construction of a will was at issue in *Lane* v. *Vick.* Justice John McLean held that, despite the "greatest respect" due state court decisions, "the mere construction of a will" where no statute was involved did not "constitute a rule of decision for the courts of the United States." McLean's opinion cited *Swift* and was supported by Justice William Johnson's dissent in *Daley* v. *James* some 20 years before, but was not strictly within the meaning of "general commercial law" as stated by Story in 1842. In part for this reason, John McKinley, joined by Roger Taney, dissented. McKinley acknowledged that federal jurisdiction was written into the Constitution to give plaintiffs "a tribunal, presumed to be free from any accidential state prejudice or partiality." But, recalling the strict presentation of the rule pronounced in *Swift,* McKinley exclaimed that questions involving wills should be governed by the local law. This was necessary to avoid a contest between state and federal courts, and out of "obedience" to section 34.[5]

Two years later the Court displayed a more striking disregard of state law in *Rowan* v. *Runnels.* This decision was only an indirect application of *Swift,* though it did seem to represent an extension of the federal judiciary's discretionary judgment over local law. The complicated facts of the case raised the question whether the Supreme Court was bound by a Mississippi supreme tribunal's interpretation of the state constitution and a statute enforcing a provision of that constitution. A Virginia creditor sued a Mississippi debtor on a contract involving a sale of slaves. The transport of slaves into the state for sale had been prohibited by the constitutional provision, but the act enforcing the provision was passed after the contract was made. The Virginian claimed that the constitutional and statutory prohibition in effect created a retroactive impairment of his contract, but neither the state or lower federal court accepted this argument.[6]

Upon appeal to the Supreme Court, however, the creditor had better luck. Chief Justice Taney noted that federal courts owed comity to state tribunals "upon the construction of their own constitution and laws." But this comity did not apply where it would bring about a nullification of a legitimate contractual obligation. While he mentioned the contract clause of the United States Constitution, Taney based the Court's decision on authority implied in the grant of judicial power in Article III. The chief justice emphasized that the Virginian's contract had been made before the Mississippi legislature had passed the law implementing the constitutional prohibition against the slave trade. Because one of the major reasons for creating the federal judiciary had been to protect the rights of nonresident creditors, the Court would not, Taney exclaimed, give the statute "a retroactive effect . . . For, if such a rule were adopted, and the comity due state decisions pushed to this extent . . . [the] provision in the Constitution . . . which secures to citizens of another state the right to sue in the courts of the United States, might become utterly useless and nugatory." Only Daniel dissented to Taney's interpretation of Article III.[7]

In 1850 the limits of federal judges' discretionary authority over state law became still more unclear. In *Williamson* v. *Berry*, a divided court refused to follow several New York decisions construing a private act of the legislature that had been passed to relieve a debtor. James Wayne speaking for four other justices held that the federal courts were free to ignore the state decisions and to determine for themselves the interpretation of the private acts. To this proposition Nelson, joined by Taney and Catron, dissented. Nelson, a former member of the New York Supreme Court, argued that the Court was "indirectly" exercising a power "where no such power exists directly under the Constitution or laws of congress . . . [and for which] there is no limit . . . except the discretion and judgment" of the Supreme Court. In the same year the Court deferred to an Alabama law controlling commercial transactions in *Withers* v. *Greene*. This case concerned a debt between citizens of Alabama and Tennessee in which there was evidence of fraud. The Alabama statute gave debtors the use of fraud as a defense even though the note giving rise to the debt had been assigned to an innocent third party. Justice Daniel admitted that where no statute existed the law governing the transaction would be the general commercial law. But since there *was* an act of the legislature, Daniel held that in this case it must provide the rule of decision.[8]

The Williamson and Greene decisions suggested a troubling uncertainty in the minds of the justices as to the limits of their authority over state law. In 1850 Chief Justice Taney, attempting perhaps to reduce the confusion, restated the original *Swift* formula on circuit in *Meade* v. *Beale,* but problems continued. Five years later in *Pease* v. *Peck,* under somewhat peculiar circumstances, the Michigan Supreme Court overruled 30 years of settled decisions construing a statute of limitations. When out-of-state litigants brought the issue before the United States Supreme Court, the majority refused to follow the new rule, adhering instead to the old line of settled precedents. "On a sudden" and by "retroaction," the Court held, the Michigan decision "destroys vested rights of property of citizens of other states, while it protects the citizens of Michigan from the payment of admitted debts." This brought the "interests of citizens of other states . . . directly in conflict with those of the citizens of Michigan." In such cases it was the Court's duty, under the Constitution and laws of Congress, to enforce the "right" of non-residents to an "unbiased judgment." In dissent new Associate Justice John Campbell, joined by Daniel, argued that the question was "so entirely of a domestic character, and belongs so particularly to the constituted authorities of the state to determine, that I cannot bring myself to oppose their conclusion on the subject."[9]

Campbell became a persistent defender of state law in federal court. In 1855, the same term in which he dissented in the Peck case, Campbell wrote a powerful unanimous opinion upholding local law in *Beauregard* v. *The City of New Orleans.* This case involved title to real estate in the Crescent City where creditors were disputing a debtor's claim to it. Louisiana law favored the creditors and Campbell made it the rule of decision. Federal courts, he said, "administer the laws of the State and to fulfill that duty they must find them as they exist in the habits of the people, and in the exposition of their constituted authorities. Without this, the peculiar organization of the judicial tribunals of the states and the Union would be productive of the greatest mischief and confusion." Consistent with these views, the justice dissented in the same year to Taney's refusal to follow a state law that constituted a "retroactive" impairment of contract in *Dodge* v. *Woolsey.* And near the very end of his tenure on the Court, shortly before the Alabaman joined the Confederate forces, Campbell wrote a majority opinion which overruled the Court's stand taken regarding state law in *Williamson* v. *Berry*.[10]

Campbell's dissents and opinions suggest how far the members of the Supreme Court were from a consensus concerning the status of local law in federal court. The case of *Watson* v. *Tarpley* in 1856, however, revealed that agreement was possible where the commercial law was in question, though ironically, this agreement would only obscure further the status of the *Swift* doctrine. In this case a citizen of Tennessee sued a resident of Mississippi on diversity jurisdiction for recovery on a bill of exchange. A Mississippi statute favored debtors in such cases, and the defendant relied upon it. But Daniel (the author of *Greene*, and dissenter in *Rowan*) and a unanimous Court (including Campbell) were not impressed. The general commercial law was neither bound by "local limits" nor its administration confined to a "particular jurisdiction." The Constitution and laws of the United States, said the justice, gave to federal court the power to uphold the contractual rights of nonresidents where they were "defined by that general commercial law." And "it must follow by regular consequence," he continued, that any state law or regulation, "the effect of which would be to impair the rights thus secured, or to divest the federal courts of cognizance thereof . . . must be nugatory and unavailing." The extent to which the Mississippi statute either subverted rights under the commercial law or impaired federal power of enforcing them was, therefore, "without authority and inoperative." Any state law which had this effect was, Daniel concluded, "a violation of the general commercial law, which a state would have no power to impose, and which the courts of the United States would be bound to disregard."[11]

The unanimous *Tarpley* decision revealed that a subtle transformation had occurred in the conception of the *Swift* doctrine by the late 1850s. Story's opinion as originally stated held that section 34 bound federal judges to follow state law where statutes, established local customs, and judicial constructions of these were at issue—but not in cases involving the general commercial law. The *Carpenter* decision, judgments by a majority of state supreme courts, and commentary by Hare, Parsons, Wallace, Kent, and others support the view that this conception of federal judicial authority was acceptable to contemporaries through the 1840s and 1850s. In *Withers* v. *Greene* Daniel was faithful to the original formulation of the *Swift* doctrine in deferring to a state statute (even where the commercial law was at issue) and Campbell's *City of New Orleans* decision holding that federal courts must follow local law in questions involving real estate was also consistent with Story's opinion. These decisions were unanimous, suggesting that as late as 1855 (the date of Campbell's *City of New Orleans* opinion) the members of the Court, like many state judges and legal commentators, accepted the basic form of the *Swift* doctrine, as stated in 1842. What explains, then, *Watson* v. *Tarpley*, a decision in which the Court justified ignoring a state statute on the grounds that it violated the general commercial law?

A consideration of the cases in which the Court's refusal to follow local law met with dissent, may help answer this question. Dissents occurred in *Vick, Berry, Peck,* and *Runnels.* In each of these cases the ultimate question dividing the Court was the propriety of refusing to follow local law in order to protect the creditor and property rights of nonresidents. The majority, of course, supported the rights of the out-of-state citizens, while the minority attached a higher value to limiting the discretionary authority of federal judges. The voting record of the dissenters reveal that they supported the initial form of the *Swift* doctrine or some application of it, but could not sanction its particular use in specific cases. Daniel concurred in *Swift* and *Carpenter,* wrote the *Greene* decision, dissented in *Runnels,* but voted with the majority in *Vick,* and wrote the *Tarpley* opinion. Taney concurred in *Swift* and *Carpenter,* dissented in *Lane,* but wrote *Runnels,* and on circuit expressed his approval of *Swift* in

Meade v. *Beale*. Even Campbell, who authored *The City of New Orleans* and the second *Berry* decision in 1860, dissented in *Peck*, but joined the unanimous decision of *Tarpley*. Nelson, dissented in the first *Berry* decision, but concurred in *Peck* and *Tarpley*. This strongly suggests the conclusion that throughout the 1840s and 1850s the members of the Court believed that the *Swift* doctrine was a proper exercise of federal judicial authority, but could not agree upon limits to its use.

If by the mid-1850s the Court was having difficulty in agreeing upon the limits of the *Swift* doctrine, *Tarpley* may have represented an effort to reestablish some consensus. Samuel Nelson, Benjamin R. Curtis, Robert C. Grier, and John A. Campbell had come to the Court since 1842. More important, perhaps, was the persistent need on the part of Taney and his colleagues during the 1840s and 1850s to reconsider and reshape the doctrines governing federal-state relations developed by Marshall. Taney strove to develop a constitutional theory that would retain effective authority in the national government and the federal judiciary, while emphasizing the role of the states as full partners in the federal system. In cases involving the commerce power, admiralty, jurisdiction, debtor-creditor rights, and other questions, Taney and a majority hammered out such a theory.[12]

Tarpley may be viewed as fitting into this mold. Given the unanimity of the Court in this case, it seems that all the justices (including those new members such as Campbell) accepted the basic proposition that there was a general commercial law that was ultimately the expression of general principles common to the entire mercantile world and distinct from local jurisprudence, as stated in *Swift*. The theory of the *Tarpley* decision differed, of course, from that of *Swift* in that the Court sanctioned its use of the general law with reference to the Constitution, and in doing so refused to follow a statute. This transformation in legal theory in effect gave the concept of "general law" a standing equal to the Constitution itself. But it also provided the Court with a device whereby it could blunt the operation of state statutes dealing with commercial contracts, without raising the question of the constitutionality of these laws. Daniel had used his theory to explain why the federal court was "bound to disregard" the Mississippi statute; he did not invalidate the statute as an unconstitutional exercise of state power. This meant that the law could continue to operate on local residents, but would not be allowed to violate the rights of out-of-state creditors. Thus, *Tarpley* was consistent with other decisions of the Taney Court in that it attempted to balance the authority of federal judges to protect nonresidents, with the recognition that local law was supreme in its sphere.[13]

This view receives support from the fact that following the depression of 1839–1843 states began passing statutes designed to regulate commercial contracts. Before the emergence of this trend, as we have seen, development of commercial law had been left to the courts. In such an environment Story's view that state court decisions were merely evidence of what the law would be without them (and as such were not binding on federal judges) had not run afoul of the state legislatures' power. *Withers* v. *Greene* represented a willingness by the Court to accept a local statutory rule which defeated the claim of an out-of-state citizen (though it may have done so in part because the case involved fraud). By 1856, however, it may have become apparent that the threat to nonresident-creditor rights was significant enough that recourse to the Constitution seemed necessary. *Tarpley* therefore could have represented the Court's attempt at infusing the notion of general commercial law with constitutional theory in order to blunt the growing influence of state laws.[14]

By the Civil War, a pattern characterizing the evolution of the *Swift* doctrine had emerged. The Supreme Court (and informed contemporary opinion) accepted the doctrine as representing a legitimate use of power necessary to the protection of interstate transactions. The members of the Court concurred in supporting the original formulation of the Swift doctrine, but they were unable to agree on limits to its application beyond the commercial law. They were unanimous, however, in accepting a transformation of the original *Swift* principle by holding in *Watson* v. *Tarpley* that the Constitution implicitly sanctioned the general commercial law, thus giving federal judges the power to ignore state statutes in cases involving commercial contracts. This decision suggests that the justices of the Court continued to believe that mercantile principles were evidence of universal standards of business behavior reflected in the jurisprudence of the nation and the world. But Campbell's dissents (emphasizing as they did the importance of local custom and conditions in determining rules of law) revealed a growing attention to the idea that the only real source of legal principles was the law of the state. As this idea came to dominate legal thought, it became apparent that the notion of general law was irreconcilable with the theory of the supremacy of state jurisprudence. This change in legal thinking became the central theme of the history of the *Swift* doctrine after 1860.

During the Civil War and Reconstruction the spread of the *Swift* doctrine was part of the general expansion of federal judicial authority that characterized the period. Congressional willingness to enlarge the diversity jurisdiction of the federal courts was a significant factor in federal judges' increasing recourse to the doctrine. In 1867, because of Reconstruction and various challenges to the freedman's rights, Congress extended diversity jurisdiction to cases where local prejudice reduced the chances of a fair trial. These cases were removeable to the lower federal courts from state tribunals. In 1875 Congress enlarged the right of removeability and the limits of diversity jurisdiction to the limits permitted by the general terms of Article III of the Constitution. The Supreme Court in 1877 construed this new law to include corporations. The Act of 1875 opened the lower federal court to a "flood" of corporate litigation.[15]

The willingness of Congress to enlarge federal jurisdic-

tion contributed to a transformation of the national economy. By 1870 the specialized middlemen who had dominated American business since the end of the War of 1812
were being displaced by large-scale corporate enterprise.
The rise of this new economic order involved fundamental
changes in technology, marketing, and managerial organization. Law and legal institutions both facilitated and
impeded the growth of this interstate corporate economy.
Many state legislatures passed laws designed to curb or prevent altogether the local operation of nonresident railroads,
manufacturing firms, and insurance companies. State courts
often sanctioned these efforts, frustrating not only the narrow self-interest of the corporations but creating a real im-
pediment to the development of the national economy. As
they had before the Civil War, federal courts provided national business interests a forum more removed from local
uncertainty and prejudice. A major incentive for removing
a case from state to federal court was the availability of the
general law. Commenting upon the newly passed Removal
Act of 1875, the editor of the *Monthly Western Jurist* candidly
explained how the federal courts' independent judgment
could affect a litigant's choice of forum. Under the enlarged
jurisdiction of the new law a nonresident insurance company could seek "the most favorable construction of . . . its
contract . . . by choosing the tribunal which suited . . . it
best." A policy holder, the editor continued, "insuring in a
company from another state, became . . . liable to have his
case adjudicated upon by the Federal courts, whether he
likes it or not. He cannot rely on the decisions of the state
in which he lives . . . for the case can be removed to the
Federal court . . . [unless] his policies are in home companies." [16]

But congressional action was only one factor in the
spread of the *Swift* doctrine. From 1860 on, judges of the
lower federal courts displayed a willingness to apply the
"general law" in a growing number of cases. Justice Stephan
Field, riding circuit in California, revealed his view of the
doctrine in *Galpin* v. *Page.* This case involved a nonresi-

dent's claim to land located in San Francisco. Field stated that the federal courts, while not foreign courts in relation to those of the states, were "courts of a different sovereignty, exercising a distinct and independent jurisdiction," and were no more "bound" by California state court decisions than the tribunals of other states. This was the "true" and "only doctrine . . . consistent with any just protection to the citizens of other states." Given the "constant intercourse between citizens of different states" any other policy would cause "the greatest insecurity to property . . . [and] would become the frequent instruments of fraud in the hands of the unscrupulous, and be sprung on the property of the unsuspecting."[17]

The Supreme Court also continued to enlarge the "general law," despite state court decisions and statutes to the contrary. Justice Samuel Miller's opinion for a unanimous Court in *Yates* v. *Milwaukee* in 1870 was an example of this process. A Wisconsin statute authorized the city of Milwaukee to prevent any building that might obstruct the free flow of a river. Applying its view of the law, the city attempted to remove a wharf built by a private citizen. Involved in the case was a decision by the Wisconsin Supreme Court denying the wharf's owner a riparian right to build into the river. When the city contracted to have the wharf destroyed, the owner petitioned the federal court for a restraining order against the contractor. The federal judge followed the Wisconsin decision and upheld the city. The wharf's owner appealed to the Supreme Court, where Miller held that the riparian right was "property" and was "valuable," and when "once vested" it "can only be deprived in accordance with established law, and . . . taken for the public good, upon due compensation." And what law determined the rule controlling the federal court? The law governing the federal judges was established by "general principles" of the common law. In such cases, Miller said, "this court has never acknowledged the right of State courts to control our decisions, except perhaps, in a class of cases where the state courts have established by repeated decision, a rule of property in regard to land titles particular to the state." Thus, upon "general principles" of common law the wharf's owner won.[18]

By the 1880s the general law included 26 distinct doctrines. The two main categories of cases in which this enlargement took place involved tort liability in accidents and recovery on defaulted municipal bonds.[19] *Gelpcke* v. *Dubuque* in 1864 was the decision that established the Court's policy toward the bond cases. This case raised the question whether federal courts were bound by Iowa Supreme Court decisions construing the state's constitution and laws. The Constitution of 1850 prohibited the state or municipal governments from becoming stockholders in any private corporation. But during the 1850s, in response to railroad pressure and local enthusiasm for development, the legislature passed laws giving localities the authority to float bonds in order to attract railroads and manufacturing firms. By the 1860s, however, many of these schemes had collapsed forcing the municipal governments to default, leaving the bondholders with nothing. Many of the creditors had in fact purchased the bonds as speculative investments while others had been involved in fraud, but these considerations did not prevent numerous suits against many of Iowa's communities. When the bondholders sued in the popularly elected local courts the results were predictable. Upon appeal to the state supreme court (whose members were also elected) numerous precedents were overruled in order to support the constitutionality of the localities' repudiations.[20]

The creditors then turned to the federal courts. The *Dubuque* case gave the United States Supreme Court the opportunity to address the issues raised by the bond repudiations. Justice Noah Swayne acknowledged that federal courts were bound by local law wherever it applied, but where the question involved the commercial law, he said, federal judges were free to apply an independent judgment as to rules of decision. Swayne stressed that there were conflicting precedents in Iowa's local law concerning the legitimacy of the debts; a large number of early decisions interpreted the state constitution so as to deny the legality of the repudiations, whereas recent opinions had overruled these cases and established the opposite principle. Could the Supreme Court remain loyal to its constitutional charge to protect contracts if it followed "every oscillation" of the state court's decisions? It was true, Swayne said, that federal courts were bound to follow state decisions construing the state's own statutes and constitution, he concluded, "But there have been heretofore, in the judicial history of this court, as doubtless there will be hereafter many exceptional cases. We shall never immolate truth, justice, and law because a state tribunal has erected the altar and decreed the sacrifice."[21]

Swayne based the Court's refusal to follow the Iowa decisions on the Constitution's charge to protect creditor rights and the general commercial law (he said the bonds were commercial contracts within the meaning of the general law). This reasoning combined that used by Taney in *Runnels* in 1847 with that stated by Daniel in *Tarpley* in 1856. But the opinion also explicitly claimed the right to apply an independent judgment in cases where the local law was unsettled, threatening "truth, justice, and law." On the whole the *Dubuque* decision represented a significant extension of federal judicial authority over state law, and Miller refused to sanction this extension in a vigorous dissent. He admitted that the Court had made exceptions in its obedience to local law, but in this case the "advance is in the direction of a usurpation of the right which belongs to the state courts to decide as a finality upon the construction of state constitutions and state statutes." The consequence of this was "not now possible to foresee," he warned, but it was clear that "we have two courts sitting within the same jurisdiction, deciding upon the same rights, arising out of the same statute, yet always arriving at opposite results." There was "no hope" proclaimed Miller, "of avoiding this if this court adheres to its ruling."[22]

It seems unlikely that Miller disagreed with the basic conception and application of the general law, since he used it

himself in *Yates* v. *Milwaukee* in 1870, and in other cases.
But there was little doubt that Swayne's *Dubuque* decision
represented an extension of the *Swift* doctrine that Miller
believed posed grave consequences for the harmonious operation of the federal system. Behind the concern for conflicts arising between state and federal courts in cases involving the same facts in the same jurisdiction was probably
his fear that local taxpayers (in order to pay off the con-
tested bonds) would become insurers against the poor judgment or fraudulent practices of municipal officials. This violated his deeply held conviction that public officials should
exercise fiscal responsibility; it also represented an unwillingness to sanction creditor claims that were often based
upon speculation and sharp dealing.[23]

Whatever the actual considerations behind Miller's dissent, it soon became apparent that his prophecy of a "contest" arising between state and federal courts had come to
pass. During the 30 years after the *Dubuque* decision, ap-
proximately 300 bond cases came to the Supreme Court
(more than on any other single issue), while many others
were settled in the lower federal courts without appeal. The
financial stakes in these cases were high. One informed
observer estimated that the total of defaulted bonds across
the nation amounted to between $100,000,000 and
$150,000,000. Resistance to creditor demands was at times
fierce. In at least one community in Missouri an angry mob
killed several judges who had signed railroad bonds regarded as fraudulent. Such anger was translated into laws
aimed at weakening the bondholders ability to recover.
Iowa and other states attempted to deny railroads and other
nonresident corporations the right of doing business within
the state unless they agreed not to remove litigation into
federal courts. Often, local officials charged with enforcing
the creditors' rights resigned rather than carry out court
orders directing the localities to levy taxes to pay off the
debts. There were instances of counties reorganizing themselves in attempts to escape payment. State judges, sensitive
to their public standing as elected officials, generally sanc-

tioned or ignored these efforts, thereby favoring debtor over creditor rights.[24]

But in most instances the states' efforts were in vain. The Supreme Court did let stand some bond defaults where the rights of nonresident creditors were not at issue, but in the majority of cases local governments were ordered to cover the debts. Time and again, as the bond cases came to the Supreme Court throughout the late nineteenth century, the justices were faced with statutory and constitutional provisions that had been interpreted by state judges in favor of the localities. As it had in *Dubuque,* a majority of the Court refused to follow the state decisions, basing their opinion on "general principles," authority implied in the Constitution, and the moral rectitude of defending the rights of creditors. In *Town of Venice* v. *Murdock* in 1875 Justice William Strong repeated the standard line: The claim that state decisions were "judicial constructions of a state statute . . . [would] have force," he said, "if the decisions, in fact, presented a clear case of statutory construction; but . . . they are not attempts at interpretation. They assert general principles." Noting the "dishonesty" of many attempts to avoid paying debts, Strong affirmed that the Supreme Court's moral duty in such cases was to defend creditor rights.[25]

Miller, often joined by Field and David Davis, consistently dissented in the bond cases. These dissents, however, seem not to have represented a rejection of the fundamental notion of general law, as much as an unwillingness to sanction its application in particular instances. This view is supported by the fact that Miller and Field used the doctrine in other cases and is reenforced by the unanimous decision of *Burgess* v. *Seligman* in 1882. *Seligman* did not involve bonds but raised the question whether stockholders of a corporation at its dissolution were liable for its debts. The issue arose in Missouri where a statute regulated the liability of corporations in such cases; the Missouri Supreme Court had construed the law against the stockholders (but after the case was begun in the federal circuit court). The United States Supreme Court held that it was "not bound to follow the decision." Joseph Bradley's opinion was perhaps the clearest statement since *Swift* v. *Tyson* of the Court's conception of its authority to ignore or follow the local law. Bradley admitted that rules establishing rights to property are regarded as "authoritive declarations of what the law is. But where the law has not been thus settled, it is . . . [the federal judges'] right and duty to exercise their own judgment." The sorts of cases in which this independent judgment was necessary and proper included those involving "commercial law and general jurisprudence," and those in which rights to contracts had "accrued" based upon long established local precedent, even though a "different interpretation may [have been] given by the State courts after such rights [had] accrued."[26]

The fact that the *Seligman* decision was unanimous suggests that the Court had arrived at a consensus as to the limits of its authority over state law. This unanimity, like that present in *Yates* (1870), occurred after years of dissent from Miller, Field, and others. Approached in this light, Bradley's opinion reveals how the members of the Court had come to view the general law and their authority for its expansion by the early 1880s. The justices apparently agreed that it was proper in certain cases to refuse to follow state law where the defense of creditor and property rights was at stake. The disregard of local law was justified on the grounds that the intent of the grant of judicial power in the Constitution was the preservation of the rights of parties to interstate transactions. But this implied constitutional duty rested upon a concept of law according to which all court decisions were either inaccurate or "authoritative declarations of what the law is." The duty of all courts was to declare the true law, but federal judges were governed in their determination by the Constitution itself, and any decision contrary to the intent of the Constitution was, as Daniel had said in *Watson* v. *Tarpley*, "inoperative." Bradley's *Seligmen* decision may have been the Court's attempt at synthesizing the theories developed in *Swift*, *Runnels*, *Tarpley*, and *Dubuque* into a single doctrine that federal judges might apply with certainty. If this was so, it was an effort doomed to failure, as decisions involving accident liability revealed.

The common law included two doctrines regulating the liability of employers for the negligent acts of their employees. The first held that employers were exempt from liability for accidents resulting from the negligence of employees except in a limited number of cases. The other rule, however, enforced a broad range of responsibility for the conduct of an employer's agent. The two variations of the legal doctrine grew in part out of different stages of technological development in England and the United States, but its evolution was also greatly influenced by more complex cultural factors. These factors involved an end to the use in tort cases of a technical legal form known as the writ system, and a change in the character of this litigation from cases involving primarily persons having a close relationship with one another to cases involving strangers. Behind these elements was the emergence after 1850 of a major transformation in American intellectual life, including legal scholars, that stressed "scientific" analysis of the human condition and urged the substitution of secular theories for religious dogma. With these forces at work, state courts by mid-century tended to favor the more liberal rule, though there was in fact no unanimity across the country. In 1860, the Wisconsin Supreme Court gave its reasoning for supporting the liability of employers. "Public policy requires that the employees of a railroad company should receive the same protection against injury by other employees, which the law affords to every other person," the court said, "for if the liability of the employer for the negligence of his servants is reduced, so the motives will be diminished which induce him to employ servants of the greatest skill and vigilance, and the hazard of the public will be increased thereby."[27]

The federal courts provided a unique function in the development of the fellow-servant doctrine and other rules governing accident liability. They provided railroads and other interstate corporate businesses a forum more removed from local uncertainty and potential prejudice against corporations. A commentator for the *Central Law Journal* in 1880 suggested that the threat of anticorporate feeling was real: "The prejudice of juries against corporations and the difficulty with which the latter can obtain what is their due, even when justice is on their side, is often commented upon." Through use of jury instructions, diversity jurisdiction, and the general law, federal judges (much as they had in commercial litigation) were able to develop in some measure an apparent consistency of doctrine administered in federal courts.[28]

This consistency was more apparent than real and emerged gradually between the 1860s and 1890s, but the tendency of the Supreme Court at least was toward rules favoring a limited employer liability. Circuit judge David Brewer (who would become associate justice of the Supreme Court in 1890) expressed an opinion on the subject shared by other federal judges. No rule should "be construed," said Brewer, "as lifting . . . a single subordinate, into the dignity of a departmental director. We should . . . not dignify with undue importance . . . a mere regulation of details." That an employee's actions might create the "possibilities of disaster . . . do not make him . . . the representative of the master." The employee's "duties should be principally those of direction and control. He should be so lifted up in the grade and extent of his duties, as to be fairly regarded as the alterego—the other self—of the master."[29]

The drift toward Brewer's position began in 1862 with an enlargement of the general law to include tort cases. *Chicago v. Robbins* in that year involved the liability of a New Yorker who owned an urban lot in the Windy City. His contractor had, despite repeated warnings from city officials, neglected to maintain a safe construction cite, resulting in the injury of a passer-by. The city sued the New Yorker in state court where he was able to remove the case to the federal circuit court. The federal tribunal followed Illinois precedent ruling in favor of the non-resident. The city then appealed to the Supreme Court. Justice Davis for the majority noted that a "case of grosser negligence could hardly be imagined," and held that the lower federal court had been wrong in following Illinois law. While state law bound federal courts where "rules of property . . . are fully settled," concluded Davis, in cases where "private rights are to be determined by the application of common law rules alone, this court, although entertaining for state tribunals the highest respect, does not feel bound by their decision." With Nelson and Miller in dissent (without opinions) the Court reversed the lower federal court and upheld Chicago on the merits.[30]

In *Robbins* the Court refused to follow the local law on the basis of the *Swift* doctrine, but did so in order to uphold the liberal doctrine. English and American courts tended to follow the liberal rule where an agent's negligence resulted in an injury to an innocent bystander. By the early 1880s, however, the Supreme Court and some lower federal courts seemed unwilling to extend a similar protection in cases involving injuries to fellow servants. Then, in 1884 in *Chicago, Milwaukee & St. Paul R. Co.* v. *Ross,* Field led a five-to-four majority in extending employer liability to include injuries to fellow servants caused by the negligence of train conductors. An engineer of a railroad engine was badly hurt due to the negligence of his supervisor, a conductor. Field held that the conductor was "the representative of the Company, standing in its place and stead in the running of the train . . . [and the engineer] was . . . his subordinate, and that for the former's negligence, by which the latter was injured, the company was responsible." Bradley's dissent refused to sanction the "breakdown" of the "long established rule" exempting employers from "injuries to their servants by the negligence of their fellow servants."[31]

The five-to-four vote in *Ross* suggests that the issue raised was not an easy one for the Court to decide. In fact, decisions of the Supreme Court and the federal circuit courts for the next eight years revealed a marked inability of federal judges to agree upon the limits of the *Ross* doctrine. On circuit in 1885 Miller (who had voted with the majority the

year before in *Ross*) acknowledged the extent of controversy
and the clash of values upon which it rested. Exclaiming
that there was "no unanimity in the decisions of courts nor
in the opinion of the profession," Miller concluded that it
was his "personal judgment, as a matter of sound principle"
that *Ross* should govern the present case. He stressed the
"length of time" the Court had taken in considering the
question of employer liability and noted the "ultimate dissent" of four justices to show how important the resolution
of the issue had been.[32]

To Miller's circuit opinion was appended a compilation of
all state precedents concerning the fellow-servant doctrine.
One James M. Kerr had apparently gathered the precedents for Miller because he signed his name at the end of
the decision. Kerr remarked, no doubt with Miller's con-
sent, that the liberal doctrine was "manifestly the only just
and equitable" one. It was good that there was a "breaking
away from the rigorous and inequitable rules of the English
common law, and from former doctrine in this country,"
Kerr concluded. The "tide seems to be now fully set in the
direction of justice and humanity, and the poor laborer,
who under the old rule was left to be driven about by the
winds of chance, stranded upon the shoals of misfortune,
or wrecked upon the rocks of adversity, will be better pro-
tected in his person and his rights in the future."[33]

Kerr's eloquent appeal for "justice and humanity" for the
"poor laborer" probably reflected Miller's convictions on the
subject. But federal judge David Brewer's circuit opinion in
1886 showed that these values were not shared by many.
This case also concerned the extension of the fellow-servant
doctrine established in *Ross*. "I think I only voice the general judgment of the profession in saying that the decision
in the *Ross Case* was a surprise," said Brewer, "and that it
carried the doctrine of departmental control to the extreme." It was not "improbable" that the principle of limited
employer liability might be "ere long . . . entirely overthrown. But if overthrown it should be by legislative action,
and not judicial decision." Brewer's preference, however,

for a narrow "departmental" responsibility did not prevent his obeying the Supreme Court's decision if precedent required. In *Borgman* v. *Omaha & St. Louis Ry. Co.* in 1890 (the same year he became associate justice) Brewer confessed that he had "heretofore had occasion to notice the embarrassments" surrounding fellow-servant cases since the *Ross* decision. But in the present case, though the issue was "not clear" in his mind, he thought that "both the spirit and reasoning of that decision compels us to hold" for the injured employee. The justice explained that he had considered the case upon "general principles," but would have followed the decisions of the state court if the question had been one of "purely local law."[34]

The Brewer and Miller circuit opinions revealed a division of opinion among federal judges concerning the fellow-servant issue and indicated how they used the general law to justify their decisions regardless of this disagreement. By the early 1890s the circuits tended to adhere to *Ross,* much as Brewer had in *Borgman,* only in so far as the facts of a given case required a strict regard for precedent. While some judges extended the employer's liability using the precedent, others did not; but they all implied or expressly stated that their decision was based upon general law. In other cases federal courts followed the local law because it "declared" what the general principle of the subject was. Thus, on the whole, the substance of the general law regarding accident liability worked out between 1884 and 1890 in the federal courts was far from clear.

The Supreme Court's decision of *Bucher* v. *Cheshire R.R. Co.* in 1887 suggests how uncertain the issue had become. The facts of the case involved recovery for an injury occurring to a railroad passenger traveling on Sunday in Massachusetts. A state statute denied the railroad's liability in such instances (in order to discourage Sunday travel) and local courts had enforced the law in a "long line of numerous decisions." The injured party, unable to get satisfaction in the state high tribunal, removed to the federal court and appealed to the Supreme Court. To complicate matters, the

Massachusetts legislature repealed the statute after the plaintiff had lost in the state courts. Miller's majority opinion stressed that the fact that injustices arose out of the operation of the state law did not "meet with the approval" of the Court, but because the law was so "long standing" the state court decisions must control the case.[35]

Miller based his decision upon the standards established in *Burgess* v. *Seligman,* noting that the numerous exceptions to the Court's deference to local law under section 34 raised an "embarrassing" question. While there was no common law of the United States, Miller explained, the "main body of the rights" of the American people were "governed by principles derived from the common law of England." It was "in regard to decisions made by state courts in reference to this law, and defining what is the law of the state as modified by the opinions of its own courts, by the statutes of State, and the customs and habits of the people, that trouble arises." Field and Harlan dissented in Miller's reasoning, arguing that the construction of the Massachusetts statute was "a question of general law upon which the federal courts were at liberty to follow their own convictions."[36]

The uncertainty evidenced in *Bucher* surrounding the inclusion of tort doctrine within the general law reached a climax in 1892. In that year, with Field (who had authored the *Ross* opinion) absent, a majority of the Court refused to apply *Ross* in *Lake Shore & Michigan Southern Railway Company* v. *Prentice.* Shortly thereafter the fellow-servant issue came before the Court again, this time with Field present, in *B. & O. R.R. Co.* v. *Baugh.* This case produced the most forceful rejection of the concept of general law since the doctrine's formulation 50 years before in *Swift* v. *Tyson.*[37]

Baugh was a fireman employed by the B. & O. when he was injured in a collision of two trains caused by the negligence of his coworker, an engineer. The accident occurred in Ohio, whose law upheld a broad employer liability in fellow-servant cases. Baugh sued in state court, but because the railroad was a Maryland corporation it was able to remove the case to the federal circuit court, which nonetheless followed the local law deciding in favor of the fireman. The B. & O. then appealed to the Supreme Court where Justice Brewer noted that the question of the relative standing of local and general law in federal court "has been often presented." But "whatever differences of opinion may have been expressed have not been on the question whether a matter of general law should be settled by the independent judgment of this court, rather than through an adherence to the decisions of the state courts, but upon the other question, whether a given matter is one of local or general law."[38]

Railroad torts were included within the general law, said Brewer, because the Constitution was created in part to regulate the commerce between the states, and the responsibility to enforce this power was left to the federal courts. Since the local law on the matter was different from state to state, how could the federal courts remain faithful to their constitutional charge if "the rights, obligations and duties subsisting between it [the railroad] and its employees change at every state line?" In order to uphold "those considerations of right and justice . . . known as the common law," Brewer concluded, it was "obvious that the relations between company and employee are not in any sense local . . . but . . . of a general nature . . . to be determined by the general rules of the common law." Refusing to follow *Ross,* Brewer held that the general law did not make the railroad liable for the negligent conduct of its fellow servants and decided against Baugh.[39]

Brewer discussed at great length the distinction between the general and local law, and the implied constitutional sanction for the former, because Field in dissent seemed to challenge the legitimacy of the entire concept. Chief Justice Fuller joined in dissent, but solely on the grounds that the facts of the case were sufficiently close to those in *Ross,* that the precedent of 1884 should have been followed. Field could not, however, "assent to the doctrine" that there was "an atmosphere of general law floating about all the states, not belonging to any of them, and of which the Federal judges are the especial possessors and guardians," and which they apply "to control judicial decisions of the state courts whenever they are in conflict with what those judges consider ought to be the law." This doctrine, he stressed, subverted the "just authority" and "autonomy and independence of the states," the supremacy of which in their proper sphere was essential to the "harmonious workings of our Federal system." That the law of the state would be enforced differently by federal courts was "never supposed" proper. As if in repentance, Field admitted that, "I confess . . . I have, myself in many instances unhesitantly and confidently, but I think now erroneously, repeated the same doctrine." Then, the penitent justice turned to the question of the applicability of the *Ross* precedent to the *Baugh* case. The majority's opinion "destroyed" the "usefulness [of *Ross*] as a protection to employees in the service of large corporations," undermining a rule that was in accord with "justice and humanity . . . [in favor of] the largest exceptions of corporations from liability."[40]

Surprisingly, Field seemed to qualify this firm rejection of the general law, by acknowledging that there was room for an independent judgment over local law in certain instances. "If a federal court exercises its duties within one of the states where the law on the subject under consideration is uncertain and unsettled," he said, "it must exercise an independent judgment thereon, and pronounce such a judgment as it seems just." Field was adamant, however, that "no foreign law, or law out of the state, whether general or special, or any conception of the court as to what the law ought to be, has any place for consideration where the law of the state . . . is settled."[41]

Baugh marked a turning point in the evolution of the Court's view of its authority over state law. Brewer correctly argued that the legitimacy of the concept of the general law had never been questioned: Dissent had always involved the issue whether the local or general law should apply in a particular case. Field's dissent, however, *did* challenge the validity of the idea of the general law. This challenge and

Brewer's defense was significant because both resorted to the Constitution in defense of each other's theory. The Taney Court had developed the policy of supporting its application of the *Swift* doctrine on the basis of authority implied in the Constitution; by the 1880s enough precedents sanctioned this policy that it was difficult to separate the concept of general law from its constitutional justification. This transformation in the theory of the *Swift* doctrine made it virtually impossible to treat federal judges' independent judgment and the conception of law upon which it rested simply (as Story had done in 1842) in terms of the construction of section 34.

As the federal judiciary continued to enlarge the body of general law so that by 1890 it included some 26 doctrines, a fundamental question arose as to the proper balance of power between the state and federal governments. This question was particularly sensitive because it involved such explosive social issues as state control over fiscal matters (the bonds), property use (riparian rights in *Yates*), and employer-employee relations (the fellow-servant cases). Behind these issues lurked a clash of values concerning the limits of local control and federal intervention and the extent of governmental responsibility for the defense of private rights, individual security, and corporate enterprise. In *Baugh,* these questions became part of a debate involving the constitutional character of the federal system itself. Given the gap between Brewer's and Field's respective views in this debate, it was unlikely (despite the attempt in *Burgess* v. *Seligman*) that the Court could agree upon either the limits or ultimate legitimacy of the *Swift* doctrine.

But *Baugh* was a turning point for another reason. Despite its forceful and repentant tone, Field's dissent explicitly stated that federal judges possessed the authority to apply an independent judgment as to rules of decision if and when the local law was "unsettled." This acknowledgement suggests that Field shared with Brewer (and probably most American judges during the late nineteenth century) the assumption that judges in fact declared what the law was rather than made it. Brewer and Field did not dispute the propriety of declaring the law; they disagreed about the source of the law they declared. Field had apparently come to accept Miller's conception of the source of law as stated in *Dubuque* and elaborated in *Bucher* that all law ultimately came from the states (or, of course, in federal questions from Congress and the Constitution). Federal District Judge Benjamin Grosscup succinctly articulated this view in a controversial decision in 1894. Such cases as *Baugh* and *Tarpley* did not, said Grosscup, show the existence of a general law, but were actually a "different interpretation" of state law by federal judges. "The decisions of the state court are not necessarily the law, but only mirrors of the law. They may be mistaken interpretations, and therefore incorrect mirrors. The litigant in federal court," concluded Grosscup, "is entitled to the law as it is, not simply to the local judicial reflection of the law."[42]

Brewer's conception of the source of law, however, was that there existed in the United States a mass of common-law principles that had been brought to America in the colonial period and adapted to changing times throughout the nation's history. This law provided the "substratum" of the law of the states, but was also something separate from any local jurisdiction. This theory had been argued by Marshall, Story, and others before the Civil War, and Field and Miller seem to have resorted to it at times. But by the 1890s this notion was developed into an argument for the existence of a national common law—extending beyond general commercial jurisprudence—and including a whole corpus of federal judge-made decisions. Antebellum federal judges had explicitly denied that they possessed authority to develop such a corpus of law following the controversy over the Alien and Sedition Acts and common-law crimes. After the Civil War, however, Brewer and others claimed that acts of Congress and the Constitution itself gave implied sanction to the formulation of a federal common law.[43]

This concept of a national common law was applied in two circuit decisions in 1894. William Howard Taft, judge of the federal circuit court in Ohio, upheld a state court's interpretation of a Tennessee statute in a fellow-servant case, but noted that if the statute had been "merely declaratory of the common law . . . such a case would be a question of general commercial law, with respect to which we might exercise an independent judgement." George Shiras (Brewer's long-time colleague on the circuit court and appointed to the Supreme Court in 1892) was more explicit in a decision aimed directly at Grosscup's source-of-law theory. The common law, as modified by the courts, the Constitution, legislation, and "changes in the business habits and methods of the people," was not derived from the states. In "all matters of national importance," Shiras said, "over which . . . control is conferred upon Congress, the courts of the United States have the right to declare what are the rules of general jurisprudence which control the given case."[44]

A divergence in the conception of the source of law evidenced in *Baugh* and the circuit court opinions suggest that a transformation in basic legal assumptions was well underway by the 1890s. Story's formulation of the general law was rooted in the conviction that mercantile jurisprudence was ultimately a manifestation of principles—universal standards of practice—common to and governing the entire commercial world. It was possible that he hoped the concept of general law would function as a theory of conflict of law, whereby federal judges would search the foreign and domestic sources of "international private law" to discover and apply the proper universal rule. The assumption of the existence of universal principles upon which general commercial jurisprudence was based seems to have been widely held by contemporaries through the 1850s (if not longer), as commentary by Parsons, Wallace, Hare, and the *Tarpley* decision suggest (though, as we have seen, other conceptions of the source of law were present in the 1820s and 1830s).

But after the Civil War, the metaphysical foundation of the belief in general standards back of all legal rules seems

to have been eroded. Undermining this belief was a growing perception that legal principles were in fact nothing
more than doctrines found in the local law of the state, or
in the national common law described by Shiras. As will become apparant, contemporaries increasingly sought to extract scientifically determined and logically consistent legal
principles from cases, rather than viewing these principles
as evidence of universal modes of mercantile behavior. As
Yates, Burgess, Bucher, and the fellow-servant cases suggest,
by the 1880s Story's conception of the basis of general law
no longer corresponded with many contemporary's views as
to the nature and source of law. Once the metaphysical
foundation of Story's concept of general law was questioned, it was reduced to the status of a formalistic legal
device. With this transformation in the assumptions behind
the *Swift* doctrine, Field and Grosscup could deny altogether the validity of the technical device, while Brewer,
Shiras, and Taft could use it to describe their formulation
of a national common law.

Between 1842 and the end of the century, the *Swift* doctrine was fundamentally transformed. Story had not
thought it necessary to discuss the constitutional implications of the federal judiciary's jurisdiction over the common
law. But, as a study of the cases show, by the Civil War
Story's mode of analysis seemed no longer adequate, for the
Court increasingly based its common-law authority on constitutional principle. This change in analytical reasoning was
important because it raised directly the very issues of federalism that a unanimous Court had apparently considered
of essentially secondary importance in 1842; it was important too because it revealed the extent to which federal
judges were unable to agree upon the limits of applying the
Swift doctrine. An initial cause of this change was perhaps
the spread of state statutes and court decisions during the
1840s, 1850s, and 1860s that threatened nonresident (especially creditor) interests. In *Watson* v. *Tarpley,* the famous
Gelpcke v. *Dubuque,* and other decisions of the period, federal judges faced questions directly involving the sovereign

power of the states. Under such circumstances, Story's theory probably seemed inadequate and the Court felt justified in linking it with the authority of the Constitution.

This seems, however, only a partial explanation. The forceful dissents of Justices Miller and Field in the bond and fellow-servant cases suggests that application of the *Swift* doctrine could stir profound disagreement. This disagreement was probably due more to an unwillingness to apply the doctrine in particular instances, than any adherence to a contrary theory of jurisprudence. But in a deeper sense, these dissents were evidence of larger changes occurring in late-nineteenth century federalism, the character of the nation's bar, and the conception of the nature and source of law. Because of these changes, controversy over the *Swift* doctrine reached beyond federal court rooms to embrace issues vital to the development of American society.

SWIFT *AND THE POSTBELLUM LEGAL PROFESSION*

Following Reconstruction, the *Swift* doctrine became the object of attempts in Congress to reduce federal judicial power. Critics argued that corporations facing local resistance and unfavorable legal doctrines would reincorporate in other states for purposes solely of creating diversity jurisdiction and gaining access to the body of general law. In other cases corporations and other nonresident creditors would assign their contracts to associates in other states in order to achieve the same result.[45] When the Removal Act of 1875 enlarged the reach of federal jurisdiction, still more nonresidents—especially corporate creditors—took their business before federal judges. The attorney general of Nebraska in 1887 pointed out one source of bitterness against the federal judiciary. If an "Eastern money-lender feels safe in loaning his money on Nebraska farms, he should be obliged to go into Nebraska courts for redress in case of violation of the contract." Whereas resistance to federal

courts had traditionally come from the South, the official
continued, "at present these complaints are made most ear-
nestly in the West and North-west where the tendency to
limit the Federal jurisdiction is certainly more outspoken
than elsewhere."[46]

Increased business burdened federal dockets, bringing
about inefficiency and delay. These developments fostered
concern for justice throughout the nation. But a writer for
the St. Louis-based *Central Law Journal* in 1884 linked the
delay and inefficiency to a threatening centralization of
power in the federal courts and a discernable preference on
the part of federal judges for corporate business. Focusing
upon the enlarged federal jurisdiction sanctioned in the Act
of 1875 (which he saw as a "danger to the interests of the
people, and gratification for corporate monopoly"), the
writer called for congressional action. There "is a well
founded suspicion that men have been elevated to the supreme judicial tribunal in the land, if not at the behest of
corporate interests, certainly with notice that . . . they
might be expected to care for their protection." The "thing
has grown. Inch by inch this centralizing influence is moving on." The writer noted further that the federal dockets
were overloaded with this litigation, often at the expense of
justice. The federal courts were often located in only one
place in the state, he pointed out, and "it is a convenient
way of exhausting one's opponent to drag him from the
northwestern county . . . and then compel him to present
this plaint to a court governed perhaps by different notions
of the law, and then . . . the suit may be ultimately carried
to Washington to be there buried for a number of years."
The critic exclaimed finally, "He who can look up these
things and not feel his State pride offended lacks elements
of patriotism. It is time to call a halt. The Federal courts
should be deprived of this power."[47]

These views received support from the fact that those engaged in interstate business expressed a clear preference
for federal courts in the trial of their litigation. Given the
"exasperating uncertainty" of jury trials, John H. Devereux

was not surprised at a verdict against his railroad in 1871, "knowing as I do," he said, "the extreme bias existing in the minds of jurors in any case wherein a corporate body is the defendent." Appellate courts were, therefore, considered more favorable to corporate interests, while deemed safest of all were the federal courts.[48] A representative of the Boston and Maine railroads, apparently having trouble fending off damage suits, suggested another reason why nonresident corporations would sue in the national tribunals. "Passengers who broke a leg would have their damage suits transferred to the United States courts," he said, "since the Boston and Maine was a foreign corporation, and if exceptions were once taken and the cause carried to the Supreme Court you die before your case is decided."[49]

A more general manifestation of these sentiments was the refusal of prominent businessmen to support possible Republican presidential candidates unless they were assured by party leaders that the candidates would appoint federal judges having "correct" views on contract and property rights. One party manager wrote James Garfield in 1880 asking him to send "privately, for my own personal use . . . your general views on this question of the rights of corporations so that I could show it to Gould and perhaps Huntington." Another party leader demanded a "prompt and careful answer" on this question from Garfield.[50] By 1894 business interest in Supreme Court appointments had not slackened. "There are so many jackasses about nowadays who think property has no rights, that the filling of the Supreme Court vacancies is the most important function of the presidential office," grumbled railroad executive Charles Elliot Perkins in that year.[51]

Disagreement over the use and limits of federal judicial power resulted in part from a transformation taking place during the late nineteenth century in the character of the nation's economy. Between the War of 1812 and the 1840s, as we have seen, specialized middlemen had come to dominate the national economic order. Following the 1870s, however, this class of merchants steadily gave up their influence to giant corporations organized on a national scale to exploit growing urban markets, an improved transportation network, and an increasingly sophisticated financial structure. By the end of the century these nationally integrated corporate organizations controlled the country's manufacturing, transportation, and commercial sectors. This transformation did not however, proceded without unrest. As industrialization worked a gradual but fundamental alteration in the nation's economic order, it contributed to a clash between local and nonresident interests. To a large degree the bond and fellow-servant cases, as well as other litigation coming to federal court during the postbellum era, arose out of disputes between local businessmen, farmers, and officials and out-of-state corporate and financial power. Both groups were seeking the benefits and facing the consequences of industrial development; both had reason to support or attack the federal courts as the defender or destroyer of their particular interests.[52]

This unrest, along with national concern for the pernicious effects of delay and inefficiency on the administration of justice, created pressure on Congress to act. Congressman David B. Culberson of Texas introduced into the house a plan intended to cut off corporate access to federal courts. The bill was originally introduced shortly after the Act of 1875 contributed to a three-or-four-year delay in hearing cases, first in the circuit courts, then in the Supreme Court itself. Culberson's bill was aimed primarily at eradicating the right of nonresident corporations to initiate suits in or remove them to the federal circuit courts. The plan proposed first that all corporations, for purposes of diversity jurisdiction, should be treated as local corporations chartered by the state. Next, these corporations should be deprived of the right of removal (on the grounds of local prejudice or another reason). Finally, the jurisdictional amount upon which access to circuit courts was based should be raised from $500 to $2000 (most fellow-servant cases, bond defaults, and other common diversity suits involved amounts under $2000). Culberson's provisions involving removal was intended indirectly to wipe out the *Swift* doctrine. Ever since the Court had construed the removal section of the Act of 1875 to include corporations, it had been resorted to in part to take advantage of the body of general law developed through an enlarged application of the *Swift* principle. If, however, the right was removed and nonresident corporations acquired the status of local entities, they would become subject to the control—and uncertainties and erratic prejudices—of local law.[53]

Between 1877 and 1896 Culberson repeatedly introduced his bill in the house. After the Texan left the Congress, others introduced like measures well into the twentieth century, but though the house usually passed these measures, the senate did not. House debates during the 1880s suggest something of the conflict of interest the Culberson bill stirred up. A congressman from Chicago explained forcefully the concern of leading Western cities for the continued support of Eastern big business, if federal jurisdiction was reduced. "Do you want to tell the merchants of the West and Southwest that . . . mercantile credits are to be obtained in the East with difficulty?" The "best guarantee" to this investment for "nearly three quarters of a century" has been the federal courts, he continued, and now it is said that recourse to them "must be withdrawn . . . and the holders of private obligations in the North and East of . . . bonds and other corporate liabilities must be remitted to state courts for their rights! A dangerous proposition . . . a bold proposition!" Due to the significance of the courts, he concluded, "Let not gentlemen deceive themselves as to the value of this security!" Merchants and lawyers in Toledo, St. Louis, Cincinnati, and other Midwestern cities no doubt shared this view, because they sent memorials to Congress condemning the Culberson plan.[54]

An Iowa representative was, however, unconvinced. "The tendency of the wealth of the country is toward associated capital. Colossal insurance companies, gigantic railroad enterprises, and other multifarious corporate organizations exist in every locality." The federal courts were the agents of corporate power, he exclaimed. They "have grown to be largely corporation mills, in which the tolls are largely taken from the individual citizen . . . it has become the fact that . . . the old feudal system . . . has sought refuge behind the judicial system."[55] What, another opponent of federal jurisdiction queried, did all this mean? It meant "the centralization of power in the Federal Government . . . [and the] obliteration of State lines and the degradation of the State judiciary."[56]

Senator (later United States Attorney General) G. H. Garland of Arkansas pointed out the connection between local control and the challenge of the *Swift* doctrine. For the "past ten or fifteen years the circuit courts, particularly in the Southern and Western States, have done little else than wreck the towns and counties and cities within their jurisdiction." In 1879, he continued, "out of the two hundred and forty-five cases on what is called the common-law side of the docket [the part regulated by Swift] of the United States court at Little Rock, one hundred and twenty-three cases were of this character."[57] Culberson summed up his views three years later. Diversity jurisdiction, removal, and the *Swift* doctrine all contributed to "swell the dockets with . . . [cases that permitted] the greatest frauds to be practiced upon the legitimate jurisdiction of these courts." The law administered in federal court, Culberson continued, "is used by corporations . . . to harass, to vex, to oppress, and especially to gain advantage over their adversaries by compelling them to litigate in courts remote from their homes with all the disadvantages attending." Finally, he concluded, "the supply of litigation from this source to Federal Courts ought to be cut off."[58]

The Davis bill represented the Senate's attempts at eliminating delays and inefficiency in the federal judicial system. Introduced for the first time in 1877, it proposed a major restructuring of the federal judicial system by creating a new level of intermediate appellate courts. These new tribunals would become the final courts of appeal in a large number of cases that under the existing system would go to the Supreme Court. Appeal to the Supreme Court was possible, but narrowly circumscribed. Unlike the Culberson scheme, the Davis bill simply called for administrative reform and evidenced little or no suspicion of corporate power. The senate and house plans did for many years, however, have one thing in common: Neither were enacted into law because of congressional wrangling. "No measure increasing the number of Federal judges could be gotten through," lamented the *Central Law Journal* in 1885, "because the new appointments would inevitably be selected" by the majority party. The result was a deadlock, which constituted, the journal concluded, "a very great shame." This party wrangling even reached the point that Democrats charged Republicans that federal judges (many of whom had been appointed during periods of Republican rule) selected only citizens from their own party to sit on juries.[59]

But by the late 1880s Democrats and Republicans in both the house and senate could no longer resist pressure for reform. The Culberson proposals never became law in their extreme form, but in 1888 the House and Senate agreed to a compromise measure that at least reduced somewhat the grounds for removal of cases from state to federal court for reasons of local prejudice. Even in this diluted form, the *Central Law Journal* proclaimed that the new law was as significant as the Interstate Commerce Act passed the same year. Four years later the burden on justice created by congested federal dockets forced congressional partisanship to abate further. In 1891 bipartisan support in both houses passed a revised version of the Davis bill, establishing a new system of appellate courts. The new law virtually ended the circuit riding of justices of the Supreme Court and eliminated the heretofore common occurrence of cases being tried and appealed by the same federal judge.[60]

As comments by Garland and Culberson show, opposition to the *Swift* doctrine was a major factor behind Congressional efforts to limit federal jurisdiction. The fact that lawyers joined merchants in petitioning Congress in support of federal judicial power suggests, however, that there were members of the bar who favored *Swift*. A Charleston lawyer named Edward McCrady in 1876 implied such a view: "the bar of this section of the country are much inclined to take their cases into the United States courts, and the dispatch of business in those courts is . . . a matter of [great] concern to us." The report of the committee of the American Bar Association charged with considering reform of the federal judicial system in 1882 was more explicit in its concern for the viability of the *Swift* doctrine. Noting that interstate business had "immensly expanded" after the Civil War, the report argued that the "spirit and intent of the Constitution" demanded protection of nonresident litigants. Fulfillment of this constitutional responsibility depended upon "the body of the common law, as administered by the federal tribunals, [which] is one of our most precious possessions. The purity and uniformity of it should be guarded with the greatest assiduity." It was the law, the report continued, "not of one state, but of all the states; not of a section, but of the entire people; not of local interests, but of the general welfare. It is the only homogeneous law we have." Given the "inevitable" differences in local law fostered by the federal system, the "whole theory and value of the federal administration of justice requires a uniformity and consistency of application before which the citizens of all the states shall be equal."[61]

Daniel M. Chamberlain, prominent New York City attorney and former governor of South Carolina, gave an in-depth defense of the *Swift* doctrine in 1889. Chamberlain examined in detail every dimension of the principle: section 34 and federalism, the *Swift* decision itself and the precedents following it, the relationship between the general law and the Constitution, and the importance of the administration of the doctrine to interstate business. The Constitution and acts of Congress recognized, the attorney said, a concurrent jurisdiction over certain litigation whereby the state and federal courts were sovereign within their respective sphere. In such a system "some anomalies . . . inconveniences . . . conflicts . . . even some abuses" where inevi-

table; though a "spirit of comity" had even reduced the occurrence of these by the late 1880s, he observed. The
former governor strongly supported Story's treatment of
section 34 and carefully traced the growth of the doctrine
through *Rowan* v. *Runnels, Tarpley,* and the "large class of
cases" involving bonds. He stressed the prevalence of confusion in the local law of the states, justifying further the
need for a uniform jurisprudence administered in national
tribunals.[62]

Much of Chamberlain's discussion was devoted to an
analysis of the constitutional rationale for *Swift* and its relevance to the interests of national business. The intent of the
Constitution's grant of diversity jurisdiction was, he said,
the creation of a forum in which nonresidents were assured
of a fair hearing. Because of the confusion and sporadic
prejudice present in the local law of many states, federal
courts could not possibly enforce their constitutional responsibility without some discretion over the formulation
and application of rules of decision. "It is a fact of everyday
observation that a resident of one State may have property
or commercial interests at the same time in several different
states," Chamberlain explained. "He may also at the same
time have agents making sales, contracts, and collections in
several other states." The "pecuniary interest" of those engaged in interstate business would be, therefore, "subject
. . . [to] many separate jurisdictions and to many discordant decisions of courts and rules of law," without the federal judiciary's maintenance of a general common law. The
former South Carolinian emphasized that no one could defend an unnecessary expansion of federal power, but neither should the "thoughtful student of our political system"
urge an end to the sanction of interstate business by federal
judges under the common law, "the only system of domestic
law co-extensive with our national boundaries."[63]

During the 1880s and 1890s other leaders of the nation's
bench and bar expressed views in agreement with Chamberlain and the ABA report. New York attorney George C.
Holt, former justice of the United States Supreme Court

Benjamin Curtis, federal circuit judge Amos M. Thayer, and one of the nation's foremost scholars of constitutional law, Thomas Cooley all sanctioned the *Swift* doctrine and the concept of general law in their writing. William Howard Taft of the federal circuit court, who had recognized the validity of the *Swift* principle in a decision in 1894, expressed his views on the general need for vigorous federal judicial power in an address before the ABA in 1895. "The capital invested in great enterprises in the South and West is owned in the East or abroad," the judge pointed out, "and corporations which use it . . . all carry their litigation into Federal courts on the ground of diverse citizenship . . . and in view of the deep-seated prejudice entertained against them by the local population, it is not surprising that they do." And, Taft concluded, noting the numerous attacks in Congress and elsewhere upon the national tribunals, "the same cause which is likely to obstruct justice for the foreign suitor creates a local feeling of resentment against the tribunal established to defeat its effect." Less candidly, law journal articles defended the theory of general law and its evolution since 1842 on the basis of precedent and authority implied in the Constitution.[64]

But a vocal and growing minority of the legal profession disagreed. During the late nineteenth century, searching criticism of *Swift* doctrine and its application by federal judges emerged in legal periodicals and law school classrooms. The *American Law Review, Central Law Journal, Southern Law Review,* and *American Law Register* published articles during the 1870s, 1880s, and 1890s that analyzed the jurisprudential foundation of the general law, concluding that its substance and meaning was "utterly illusive." Invariably, Story's opinion was presented as a major departure from Marshall's treatment of the common law in diversity cases, and Miller's dissent in *Gelpcke* v. *Dubuque* (and later Field's in *Baugh*) were presented as the only proper characterization of federal judicial authority over local law. The emphasis in each article, however, was usually upon the constitutional issue of federal-state relations raised in *Runnels,*

Tarpley, and the bond cases concerning federal judges' refusal to follow state supreme court constructions of state statutes and constitutions. Again and again these decisions were described as a "subversion" of American federalism as established in the Constitution. Ironically, the critics often agreed that the Supreme Court's protection of creditor rights was the correct "result"; they condemned, however, the reasoning used to reach it. A central assumption in the argument against *Swift* was that it erroneously established a federal judicial power over rules of decision that even Congress did not properly have under the Constitution.[65]

Perhaps the most prolific and persistent protagonist of the *Swift* doctrine was the Philadelphia lawyer William M. Meigs. Born in 1852, Meigs devoted much of his career, until his death in 1929, to the study of the federal judiciary, the Constitution, and federal-state issues. During the 1880s Meigs was called upon by supporters of the Culberson bill to give a scholarly analysis of the historical origins of the problems facing the overburdened federal courts. As part of this work he published several detailed studies of the history and development of the doctrine of *Swift* v. *Tyson.* In many ways Meig's views paralleled those of fellow critics, but in their depth and mastery of detail his researches went further than others in locating the sources of "error." To the young Philadelphian (he was 30 in 1882 when his first article concerning *Swift* was published) the constitutional issue raised by the federal judiciary's treatment of local law was part of that "nationalization which has been so persistent a symptom of our history," and which had been accelerated by the "centralizing influence" of the Civil War. Meigs attributed some "blame" for this to Chief Justice Taney, but most of the fault was due to Joseph Story's "craving appetite" for nationalization.[66]

Underlying the constitutional issue, however, was an "essential fallacy," being the "assumption of the existence of any such body of general principles" resorted to by Story as a basis for his opinion in 1842. Using these fallacious general principles, federal judges had developed an independent judgment that was in reality nothing more than their "fancy" as to what the law ought to be. Unlike other writers who condemned the federal courts on solely jurisprudential grounds, the young lawyer showed concretely that the general law fostered "forum shopping" through such devices as "colorable assignments of commercial paper in order to create diversity jurisdiction. Meigs also disagreed with critics who accepted the Supreme Court's defense of creditor rights in the bond cases (though they condemned the process by which the Courts reached this conclusion). The Pennsylvanian assumed that most of the bonds had been purchased in speculation schemes, a view that left little sympathy for the bondholder's losses.[67]

Meigs also emphasized that the delays and injustices resulting from overcrowded dockets were traceable to the advantages made possible by forum shopping. The availability of the federal tribunals as alternative tribunals to those of the states brought excessive amounts of corporate and non-resident business before federal judges that could just as well be handled in state courts. The use of the concept of general law by state judges in New York, Georgia, Illinois, South Carolina, and Mississippi further threatened the constitutional integrity of the federal system making it virtually impossible for a lawyer to adequately advise his client as to what a court may do in any given case. For Meigs, then, the *Swift* doctrine was objectionable because it represented a menacing nationalization and centralization of the federal justice, threatened to spread to the states, and finally impeded the lawyers' ability to accurately predict a court's decision based upon settled legal principle.[68]

Oliver Wendell Holmes, Jr. was another young attorney critical of the federal judiciary's treatment of local law. Just barely 31, with several years experience as editor of the *American Law Review* behind him, Holmes was asked to help edit the twelfth edition of James Kent's classic, *Commentaries on American Law*. This assignment required commentary on *Swift* v. *Tyson* and related cases in several places. Where Kent discussed the narrow legal issue of negotiability (and explicitly defended *Swift* as the best rule) Holmes seems to have accepted Story's opinion as good law. Elsewhere, however, the attorney inserted in the marginal annotations commentary that linked the *Swift* doctrine with *Gelpcke* v. *Dubuque,* and that cited Miller's dissent in the latter case with apparent agreement. This left the strong impression that Holmes accepted Story's opinion on the point of commercial law, but disagreed with the reasoning that used "general grounds of justice" as a basis of decision in the bond cases. Holmes finished the edition of Kent in 1873, about the same time that articles began appearing in legal periodicals attacking the *Swift* doctrine and its extension into new legal categories. He does not seem to have commented on the issue again until after the turn of the century (though in his law practice and in opinions written during his tenure as justice of the Massachusetts Supreme Court, he did uphold a conflict-of-law theory that was contrary to that implied in Story's *Swift* decision). Given these considerations, it is probable that Holmes' views concerning the federal judiciary's treatment of local law were similar to those expressed by other critics during the late nineteenth century.[69]

Teachers in the nation's leading law schools also expressed a critical opinion of federal judges' independent judgment and the concept of general law. James Bradley Thayer of Harvard Law School (a vigorous proponent of judicial self-restraint) argued his position in an article dealing with *Gelpcke* v. *Dubuque* appearing in 1891 in the *Harvard Law Review.* The article was written to clarify issues raised during the presentation of the *Dubuque* case in one of the student's moot courts. The "soundness in point of principle" of the *Swift* doctrine was, said Thayer, "open to question"; but the central issue of dispute was the doctrine's extension in the *Dubuque* case. The basic evil of the Court's decision in the bond case, said Thayer, was that it violated constitutional principles of federalism requiring the federal courts to adhere to the state supreme courts' construction of local law and their constitution.[70]

Ironically, Thayer consented to the result of the *Dubuque*

opinion in its defense of creditor rights. The real problem
was that the Court's decision rested in part upon the general law, rather than other, sounder reasoning. Thayer said
that the same result could have been achieved if the Court
had based its case upon the Constitution's implied grant of
authority in Article III and acts of Congress calling for the
protection of nonresidents from local prejudice. Citing with
approval the formula stated in *Burgess* v. *Seligman,* the professor noted that "absurd and irrational" actions of local
courts made the "danger to citizens of other states . . . [be-
cause of] local prejudice," a real problem. For this reason
"some power of varying from the decision of the States
must necessarily exist . . . [in the federal courts, to keep]
the local courts . . . within the limits of reason." In such
cases, federal courts could find in the local law "their own
rules of administration" which was "just assertion of power"
within the Constitution. This comparison of *Dubuque* with
the reasoning given in *Seligman* was a basic part of Thayer's
presentation of the general-law-problem in his teaching, as
student note books show. Thomas Reed Powell (who would
one day take over the teaching of constitutional law at Harvard) noted that in lecture Thayer expressed the opinion
that *Dubuque* was a "rotten" opinion whereas the later case
stated correctly the scope and nature of the federal courts'
authority. The lecture notes of Joseph H. Beale in 1886
(who would become a leading scholar on conflict of law) and
other students in Thayer's classes during the late nineteenth
century reveal a similar analysis.[71]

Another Harvard student influenced by Thayer's constitutionalism was Louis D. Brandeis. Brandeis graduated
from the law school in 1876 at the age of 19. In the years
after graduation, the future "people's lawyer" and justice of
the Supreme Court came to regard Thayer as his mentor
on the subject of American constitutional law. While no direct evidence seems to exist showing that he learned about
the *Swift* doctrine and related issues in Thayer's classroom,
information has survived suggesting that Brandeis encountered the concept of general law during his law school

years. Brandeis was a member of the Pow Wow Club, a law student organization devoted to sharpening legal skills through moot courts and other activities. In one of these moot proceedings, the employer's liability in a fellow-servant case was at issue. Discussing the New York and Massachusetts precedents relevant to the dispute (the case involved the Boston & Albany R.R. running between the two cities) Brandeis noted that a federal decision upheld a different principle than that found in the state law. As we have seen, federal judges decided fellow-servant cases on the basis of general law, and Brandeis' argument implied that he was aware of this. This experience indicates that Brandeis very early on in his legal education encountered the *Swift* doctrine, and suggests further that, like other Thayer students, Powell and Beale, he probably did not think too much of it.[72]

The faculty of the law school of the University of Pennsylvania produced some of the most searching analysis of the *Swift* doctrine and the federal authority associated with it. Francis Wharton, widely recognized scholar of international law, conflict of law, criminal law, and other subjects discussed the issue in his *Commentaries on Law* in 1884. On the whole, Wharton presented a balanced view of the concept of general law and Story's decision in particular. Sharing as he did Story's understanding of conflict of laws and international law, it was not surprising that Wharton perceived that the *Swift* doctrine could facilitate the formulation of a uniform commercial jurisprudence administered in federal court. At the same time, however, he pointed out the various inconsistencies that had developed in the local law as a result of the principle. Wharton's colleague John Innis Clark Hare, however, was more critical in his writing and teaching. Born in 1816, Hare became familiar with the growth of the common law in the United States during his tenure as editor of *Leading Cases* in the 1850s and due to his service as Philadelphia judge from 1851 to 1896. With the publication of treatises dealing with the law of contracts and constitutional law in 1887 and 1889, Hare was ranked

among the nation's leading jurists. In his teaching at the
University of Pennsylvania Law School and in his publications, Hare condemned the *Swift* principle (despite apparent acquiesence to it earlier in the editions of *Leading
Cases*).[73]

Hare's criticism was rooted in assumptions regarding the
character of the nation's constitutional order. For him, the
"first and greatest" problem of American constitutional law
was the reconciliation of local self-government with national
sovereignty. This, of course, had been a controversial issue
during the antebellum period and due to "laxity" in constitutional construction a confrontation developed resulting in
a tragic conflict. Thus, "while the fires . . . were still
smouldering" the need for a thorough reconsideration of
the nation's federal system pressed upon the American people after the Civil War. Like Thayer, Hare argued that the
state legislatures and courts were supreme in their sphere,
but the Philadelphia judge disagreed with the Harvard
scholar regarding the necessity for a limited independent
judgment where local law was "irrational." Hare refused to
countenance any discretionary authority on the part of federal judges if this meant ignoring state statutes and court
decisions as the sole source of law (except, of course, where
federal law and the Constitution were at issue).[74]

The *Swift* doctrine and its extensions in *Dubuque* and
other cases were for the jurist clear subversions of state sovereignty and the Constitution. Relying upon his knowledge
of local law, Hare pointed out that in the commercially active jurisdictions of New York and Pennsylvania the rules
followed in state and federal court concerning business matters were not the same. This condition was due to the pernicious concept of general law, which Hare believed was
nothing more than a spurious, empty form masking the
federal judges' personal opinion as to what the law should
be governing a given case. The precedents of local courts,
exclaimed the Philadelphia judge, "establish the law on a
basis which no power that is not legislative can disturb."
The application of the independent judgment in federal

court asserted a legislative authority over local private law that even Congress did not possess. "Such a result," Hare concluded, "makes the administration of justice a game, where the event depends on the skills of the players, and not on fundamental principles."[75]

Hare's treatises were compilations of lectures delivered before his classes in contracts and constitutional law. One student's notes taken in the contracts class during 1880 and 1881 reveal that at this early stage in his teaching Hare was concerned with the lack of uniformity in the local law regulating commercial contracts in his own and other states. He apparently blamed the federal court's use of the *Swift* doctrine for this state of affairs. A further indication of Hare's presentation of the *Swift* principle in the classroom was an essay written by George Wharton Pepper in 1889. Pepper (who would become a distinguished lawyer, United States senator, educator, and something of a reformer) was a student in Hare's constitutional law class where the professor's discussion stimulated his interest in the whole issue of the *Swift* doctrine. The law school sponsored an essay competition in which Pepper won first prize with *The Borderland of State and Federal Law,* an historical analysis of the concept of general law.[76]

Most of Pepper's study was devoted to a careful analysis of the categories of doctrines that had evolved since 1842 within and without the framework established in Story's opinion. The student questioned the enlargement of the *Swift* principle in the bond cases and elsewhere on the grounds that it transcended proper constitutional limits, giving federal courts power that Congress lacked. To this point Pepper's argument was consistent with Hare's views and those held by other critics of the day. But from his careful sifting of early decisions, applying conflict-of-laws theory apparently learned from Wharton's work, Pepper discovered that during the Marshall years the Court had decided cases on the basis of propositions quite close to those enunciated in *Swift* v. *Tyson.* Although he concluded that these were erroneous applications of conflict-of-laws

principles, Pepper suggested that Story's opinion may have
had a basis in ideas current during the early nineteenth century, but that because of the economic and political transformation following the Civil War, these ideas no longer
had force. For this reason, Pepper concluded, the simplest
way to end the problems generated by the enlargement of
the *Swift* doctrine was for the Court to reinterpret section
34 so as to make local law the rule of decision in all cases,
dropping forever the notion of general law. Pepper's essay
found its way into the hands of Justice Miller (the lone dissenter in *Dubuque*) shortly before his death in 1890. The old
judge commended the student's study, proclaiming that it
argued a theory close to his own convictions regarding the
Swift doctrine.[77]

By the 1890s the *Swift* doctrine had become a center of
controversy dividing the nation's bar, proponents of federal
judicial reform in Congress, the judges of the lower federal
courts, and the justices of the Supreme Court of the United
States. The American Bar Report of 1882, Chamberlain's
essay, treatises by Cooley and others, and articles appearing
in legal periodicals defending federal judges' discretionary
authority over local law seem to have represented the opinion of the leaders of the legal profession during the late
nineteenth century. The criticism of Meigs, Holmes, Pepper, and others probably embodied views that, while perhaps in ascendancy, were held by only a vocal minority. The
position of this minority, however, was strengthened greatly
by support of two of America's most prominent teachers of
law, Hare and Thayer. On the lower federal courts it was
likely that Taft and Shiras, rather than Grosscup, expressed
the mind of most circuit and district judges in favoring the
concept of general law and the increased federal power it
was used to justify. The same can be said of the Supreme
Court, as support for Brewer's majority opinion and Field's
dissent in *Baugh* show. And, of course, Culberson's very limited success in dismantling the authority built up around
Swift and diversity jurisdiction suggests that the Congress

was not overly eager to reduce the power of the federal
courts.

The scope of this debate reveals the extent to which the
issues raised by the *Swift* doctrine involved fundamental values concerning the centralization of power in the federal
government and local versus national control of the nation's
economic order. But the very fact that late nineteenth-century contemporaries came to view the *Swift* doctrine in such
controversial terms may seem puzzling when we recall that
before the Civil War the principle was twice upheld unanimously by the Supreme Court and sanctioned by commentators such as Parsons and Wallace. Even Hare apparently
abided the doctrine during the 1850s. What accounts for
his change of mind by 1880?

The impact of the Civil War itself on the thinking of
many Americans was no doubt a factor in reorienting perceptions of the wisdom and legitimacy of the *Swift* doctrine.
The preservation of the union raised new questions concerning the power of the federal government over the
states. Reconstruction, the Court's enlarged interpretation
of the commerce clause and due process clause of the Fourteenth Amendment, and the rise of federal regulation and
antitrust policy are familiar examples of a centralization of
federal power that would have been unthinkable prior to
the Civil War. The arguments of Hare, Meigs, Chamberlain, and others show that critics and defenders of the *Swift*
principle considered its spread into new areas of legal doctrine as part of a centralizing tendency that had begun before but that had greatly accelerated after the tragic struggle. Before 1860, despite a few noted exceptions, the Taney
Court applied an independent judgment over local law primarily in commercial cases, a body of jurisprudence that
even Jeffersonians had admitted was unique and therefore
subject to special treatment by federal (and state) judges.
During and after the war, however, the Court enlarged the
scope of discretionary authority to include torts, bonds, riparian rights, and more than 20 other doctrines. This re-

sulted in the creation of a comprehensive federal common law, transcending the narrow bounds established during the antebellum years.[78]

Perhaps the most controversial dimension of the postbellum growth of federal common-law jurisdiction involved its adjudication of many sorts of private disputes that were at the same time increasingly coming within the reach of state statutes. In the commerce clause and due process decisions, federal judges struck down state statutes as invalid. Decisions applying the *Swift* doctrine, however, ignored state statutes (and local court decisions construing them), thereby creating a body of jurisprudence applicable to nonresidents, but not to locals. Beginning in the 1870s, as Holmes and others showed, the debate over the *Swift* doctrine focused upon the constitutional questions raised by this development in *Gelpcke* v. *Dubuque*. As the sphere of the state legislatures' control of private rights grew after the Civil War and as federal judges developed a common law that put nonresidents out of reach of this authority, an explosive clash of sovereignties was inevitable. Thus, linked with the growing centralization of federal power during and after the Civil War, the *Swift* doctrine was seen by many as part of an "invasion by the federal government of a domain which for over a century has been regarded as within the power of the states."[79]

Paralleling this centralization of federal authority was a nationalization of the economy based upon giant corporations. The *Swift* doctrine was instrumental in the development of a national, corporate business order because it helped reduce uncertainties that localism created for the operation of interstate enterprise. But in serving this function, federal judges' use of the doctrine fostered an antipathy that linked the federal courts with the growing power of big business. Much of this antipathy was perhaps due to the fact that lawyers were able to exploit the *Swift* principle so that law was used to sanction various sharp practices and the interests of nonresidents over locals. These "discordant rules in the same locality tend to moral as well as legal dis-

order," exclaimed Judge Hare, "by giving astute practition-
ers an advantage over their more scrupulous brethren and
enabling designing men to make contracts which are understood in one sense and interpreted in another."[80]

Hare's fear of "moral as well as legal disorder" may have
reflected a concern for the character of the legal profession
and the threat of social chaos. During the antebellum period, in response to the rising clamor of Jacksonian Democracy, American lawyers gradually developed a public image
of themselves as neutral, apolitical specialists who applied
legal principles mechanically to changing human conditions. As the nation underwent the transformation from a
commercial-agrarian to a corporate-industrial economy and
as the legal profession helped shape law to this transformation, some lawyers perceived a threat to this image. By
the 1880s, fear was expressed that "gold and silver" were
undermining the integrity of the legal profession. Philadelphia lawyer Daniel Dougherty reiterated such fears in 1888.
He urged the bar to remember that their "triumphs" were
of "reason, not passion," resulting not from "genius" but
from "industry, patience, and perseverance." These values
were threatened, however, because of the "aspirations of
the age for wealth, rather than renown." Dougherty
stressed that "Trusts" were forming in "all lines of business.
If the bar yields to this craze for gold, individual character
will be lost in corporate enterprise and the bright escutch-
eon give place to the flaming sign-board. Degrade the bar
to a business, and at least some of its members will sink to
the lowest depths."[81]

Perhaps behind Hare's and Dougherty's concern was a
vague but potent feeling that the corruption of their professional image as neutral technocrats might contribute to a
rising tide of social dislocation. Urban protest and agrarian
revolt were of course salient features of the nation's development during the decades following the Civil War and the
legal profession was considered a major bulwark against anarchy. Dougherty indicated something of the level of this
feeling, warning that "Anarchy" was "openly avowed, even

under oath in the courts of justice. Fiends ready to apply
the torch and throw the bomb, who laugh at wholesale mur-
der, who would swim in gore, who abhor religion and re-
pudiate God . . . ," were gathering, he said, "in the thousands in great cities cursing the law and vowing vengeance
on its officers." As of now, Dougherty concluded, this night-
mare was "but a dark speck, [which] may e'er long cover
our skies and drench the land in blood." But with a "pure
judiciary and a bar inspired by honor, integrity, and independence, this apprehended horror . . . will pass, and our
republic will outride every gale, and bear its countless bless-
ings to distant generations."[82]

Hare's identification of the *Swift* principle with "moral
and legal disorder," then, may have involved deep appre-
hensions concerning the autonomy of the legal profession
and its role in maintaining order. Apparently defenders of
the doctrine also shared these concerns, though they viewed
Swift as a legal device that could be used to preserve those
business interests most threatened by social discontent.[83]
Thus, various social tensions may have been factors behind
the bar's increasing inability to agree upon the legitimacy of
the concept of general law and independent judgment. If
so, the change in mind between the antebellum and postbellum years concerning the *Swift* doctrine evidenced by
Hare becomes more understandable. When we consider the
impact of the war itself in forcing Americans to ponder
anew the fundamental character of the federal system, coin-
cident with the rise of big business, mass social unrest, and
the changing public image of the legal profession, it may
not seem surprising that the 1860s represented a hiatus in
perceptions of the federal judiciary's authority over local
law.[84]

But there were other factors at work during the late nineteenth century that further undermined the theoretical
foundations of the *Swift* doctrine. In the second half of the
century two schools of jurisprudential thinking worked to
undermine assumptions underlying the idea of general
commercial law. So-called analytical jurists looked to the

ideas of Bentham and Austin, conceiving of law as ultimately nothing more than the "command of some sovereign
power." The historical school (which became dominant in
the 1870s) argued, however, that the source of legal rules
was the "opinion of the community as to what is right and
expedient . . . the medium by which the moral sense of
society finds expression." Despite the heated and abstract
level of debate between the analytical and historical school,
they shared assumptions that displaced those upon which a
theory of general commercial law rested. The emphasis on
sovereignty fostered a rejection of notions that defined law
as something separate from and transcending a particular
jurisdictional authority. The historical jurists did not deny
the importance of sovereignty; they did argue, however,
that legal rules were not simply commands, but grew out of
the "mass of historical antecedents which determined how
the sovereign shall exercise or forbear from exercising his
irresistible coercive power." This focus tied all legal principles to a particular territorial unit, community, or state.[85]

The emphasis of these jurisprudential theories on sovereignty and territoriality had particular meaning for American jurists wrestling with the knotty problems of federalism
raised by the *Swift* doctrine after the Civil War. The teaching and writing of Hare and Wharton at the University of
Pennsylvania and that of Thayer at Harvard were influenced by the analytical and historical schools (though the
latter was clearly most important). The work of Chamberlain, Meigs, and others was informed by these ideas also. So
pervasive were notions concerning the source of law as
either the command of the sovereign or community custom
by the 1880s and 1890s, that it does not seem surprising
that supporters and critics used them in their analysis of the
Swift principle. Chamberlain's defense of *Swift* stressed that
"no fascinating theories of natural right and justice, nor
brilliant philosophical speculations upon the nature of society and government, but . . . a profound knowledge and
appreciation of the familiar, home-bred, hard-won, slowly-
maturing results of . . . political life and experience" were

the foundation for the Constitution and Judiciary Act of
1789 (and the portions of these documents that Chamberlain used to justify his interpretation of *Swift*). Meigs, Hare,
and others used similar reasoning in their attacks on *Swift*,
arguing that law must be found in some territorial locality
(the state); Story's construction of section 34 was, they said,
a perversion of the "true" history of the provision drafted
in 1789 and applied during the 1790s and under Marshall.
Of the critics, only Pepper's analysis suggested that history
was an unsure guide to the meaning of section 34.[86]

A revolutionary approach to legal education known as the
case method helped spread ideas associated with the analytical and historical schools. Christopher Langdell developed
and applied this method at Harvard Law School beginning
in the 1870s. Despite resistance, it was adopted by law
schools throughout the country by the end of the century.
Langdell's system was, recalled Pepper (who adopted it in
his teaching at the University of Pennsylvania Law School),
"nothing more than the laboratory method of the physical
sciences applied to the study of law." Court decisions were
treated as the "material for analysis," over which the teacher
and student "sweated" to learn the "evolution of the law."
Lectures in law school classrooms and law office apprentice-
ship were the dominant forms of legal education during
much of the nineteenth century. Because these methods
stressed the learning of established principles they challenged neither the idea of general law nor its embodiment
in the *Swift* doctrine. Pepper noted that the old system gave
the student the "answer without having to first wrestle with
the problem."[87]

The idea that law was a science was of course not new,
but its application in the case method by scholars absorbed
in the thinking of the analytical and historical jurisprudence
had a powerful influence on the minds of a new generation
of lawyers. Under the influence of these ideas teachers such
as Hare and Thayer used the case method to show that neither constitutional theory nor history provided a scientific
basis for the *Swift* doctrine. But this conviction that by

"sweating" over cases students and teachers could scientifically determine basic legal principles led to confusion in evaluating the legitimacy of the *Swift* doctrine. Thayer himself admitted in his comparison of *Burgess* and *Dubuque* that federal judges must apply an independent judgment where local law was "irrational." Equipped with this exception students went out into the world, serving corporations involved in interstate business, and no doubt found many instances in which the local law seemed irrational, at least as to the interests of their clients. In such cases the common law of the federal courts could appear more reasonable than the local law of the states.[88]

Thus by the end of the nineteenth century the dominant modes of legal thought and the prevalent method of legal education reenforced the views of both defenders and critics of the *Swift* doctrine. These forces had undermined the theoretical foundations of the idea of general law common to the whole mercantile world (upon which the original decision of *Swift* v. *Tyson* had rested). They had not, however, facilitated the formulation of a theory of the source of law that fit comfortably with accepted late-nineteenth-century notions in the same way that Story had done in 1842. As long as neither supporters nor defenders of the *Swift* doctrine were able to establish a jurisprudential rationale of sufficient power to destroy the position of the other, continued controversy was inevitable. The willingness of federal judges to develop a common law governing interstate business was no doubt another significant factor fostering disagreement among lawyers over the validity of the *Swift* doctrine. This disagreement was perhaps heightened by concerns for maintaining a favorable image of the legal profession in the public mind, and a fear of the social consequences that might arise if this image was tarnished by too intimate an association with big business.

A further complication involved the fact that since the 1850s the *Swift* doctrine had become inextricably connected with an enlarged view of federal judicial authority over state law as sanctioned by the Constitution. Contemporaries agreed that Congress did not have the power to establish rules of decision governing federal courts in cases involving local law. The question of the legitimacy of the *Swift* doctrine was, therefore, left to the Supreme Court, and, as *Baugh* showed, this was an issue a majority of the Court refused to consider. Most federal judges and a majority of the legal profession were unwilling to question the underlying theory or practical necessity of the *Swift* doctrine as long as persistent uncertainty in local law seemed to threaten the rights of nonresidents. The critics were convinced, however, that abstract principles of sovereignty and territoriality (and the issues of power associated with them) were of greater importance in determining the character of federal jurisdiction than the functional reality of localism. A troubling ambiguity remained in the perception of the proper limits of national judicial power in the federal system emerging after the Civil War.

Chapter III

Erie R.R. v. *Tompkins*

All the known guides, which have been slowly and carefully worked out over a century and a half, must be discarded and the slow, uncertain, and painful process begun all over again.

Albert J. Schweppe
"What Has Happened
to Federal Jurisprudence," 1938

Following the turn of the century, controversy over the *Swift* doctrine continued. By 1930 it became apparent that the federal judiciary's application of general law in diversity cases involved issues of such importance to the nation's federal system and legal order that action by either Congress or the Supreme Court was essential. In 1938 a divided Court handed down the decision of *Erie R.R.* v. *Tompkins,* reversing the 96-year-old precedent. As had been true of the opinion it overruled, *Erie* reflected jurisprudential assumptions and notions of sound policy prevalent during the period. Like our understanding of *Swift,* a determination of the meaning of *Erie* must take into account the general social context of which the decision was part.

MOUNTING CONTROVERSY AFTER 1900

Between the turn of the century and the Great Depression the federal judiciary continued to extend its application of the *Swift* doctrine. Judges in the lower federal courts applied their discretionary judgment as to the general law in

101

a growing number of diversity cases, amounting to about one third of all litigation arising from this source. Perhaps as much as 80 percent of this business involved corporations engaged in interstate enterprise. In order to evade the uncertainty and possible prejudice of local courts, corporations developed the practice of reorganizing in states with loose incorporation laws, solely for purposes of creating diversity of citizenship between themselves and local residents. It was common knowledge among lawyers serving these corporations that this practice enabled their clients to avoid state law when it was against them. These realities generated heated debate in Congress, legal periodicals, and law school classrooms. The critics' resistance to the enlargement of federal common law on behalf of corporate litigants was based in part on the argument that uncertainty in the local law had been virtually eradicated. The spread of state and federal regulation, the increased professionalization of legal education, the proliferation of restatements and codes, and the triumph of a national economic order during the first third of the twentieth century had removed, the critics claimed, whatever justification there had been for the *Swift* doctrine before the turn of the century. Nowhere, however, was the controversy greater than on the United States Supreme Court itself. There, a significant minority of the justices, often led by Oliver Wendell Holmes, sustained a persistent attack on the theory and practice of the *Swift* doctrine.[1]

Four cases between 1904 and 1928 revealed the extent of division on the Court. In *Muhlker* v. *N.Y. & Harlem R. R. Co.* five justices refused to apply a New York statute giving urban elevated railroads a right of way because it "invades rights to air and space" above a private property owner's easement. Holmes led four members of the Court in dissent. "We are asked," he said, "to extend to the present case the principle of *Gelpcke* v. *Dubuque.* . . . . This seems to me a great, unwarranted and undesirable extension of a doctrine which it took this court a good while to explain." It was the local law alone that gave federal courts their rule of decision in common law cases," concluded Holmes, ". . . if I am right, if we are bound by local decisions as to local rights in real estate, then we equally are bound by the distinctions and the limitations of those rights declared by the local courts." Thus, the Court should have applied the statute as binding, rather than its own view as to a general common law.[2]

In 1910, with seven judges sitting, the Court divided four to three in *Kuhn* v. *Fairmont Coal Co.* This case involved a mineral conveyance in which an Ohioan deeded away rights to subterranean coal deposits in West Virginia, while retaining possession of the surface property. The coal company began mining, causing the surface land to become "cracked, broken, and rent." The property owner sued the company in federal court. Shortly after this suit began, the state supreme court upheld the coal company in a case presenting nearly the same facts and similar issues. When the federal case was appealed, a majority of the United States Supreme Court ignored the single state decision, holding in favor of the Ohio resident on the basis of *Gelpcke* v. *Dubuque* and other opinions. Again Holmes led the dissenters. Citing the scholarship of Professor John C. Gray of Harvard Law School as authority, Holmes blasted the notion of general law and independent judgment. "It is said that we must exercise our independent judgment—but as to what? Surely as to the law of the States. Whence does the law issue? Certainly not from us." The only legitimate source of law in federal courts was the local law; there was no "general law," separate from local law of the states. "The law of a State does not become something outside of the state court and independent of it by being called the common law. Whatever it is called," Holmes concluded, "it is the law as declared by the state judges and nothing else."[3]

Division persisted, as a five-four vote in *Southern Pacific Company* v. *Jensen* in 1917 revealed. The majority struck down a worker's compensation law in favor of a railroad corporation on the grounds that it violated the Constitution's grant of admiralty jurisdiction. The majority reasoned that "general principles" of admiralty law existed common to and throughout the United States and that the New York statute conflicted with these principles. To this, Holmes responded with a powerful and eventually famous dissent. "Maritime law is not a *corpus juris* . . . ," he said. "The common law is not a brooding omnipresence in the sky but the articulate voice of some sovereign. . . . It is always the law of some State."[4]

Black and White Taxicab and Transfer Co. v. *Brown and Yellow Taxicab and Transfer Co.* was the most controversial application of the *Swift* doctrine during the early twentieth century. Two taxi companies, both Kentucky corporations, were competitors at a railroad station in Bowling Green. To quash competition, the Black and White Taxi Company made a contract with the railroad, which granted them a monopoly. Under state law, corporations incorporated under Kentucky statutes were forbidden to enter into contracts which created a monopoly. The B&W Taxi Co., in order to avoid Kentucky law, dissolved and reincorporated under Tennessee law (Tennessee being among the states having liberal incorporation statutes). The company's reincorporation was for the express purpose, as stated in the brief, of creating federal diversity jurisdiction. Once in federal court, the taxi company argued that the Kentucky provisions against monopolistic contracts did not apply to foreign corporations; they were governed instead by the law of the place of incorporation. Since Tennessee law possessed no prohibition against such contracts, the taxi company asked the federal court to ignore the Kentucky law and to enforce their contract under general principles of commercial law. The lower federal court accepted the argument and the B&W Taxi Co. won. On appeal, the Supreme Court accepted the lower court's decision. Refusing to consider whether jurisdiction was properly established, Justice Pierce Butler, exercising the prerogative power, overruled the local law and upheld the contract on principles of general law.[5]

Holmes joined by Brandeis and Harlan Stone, dissented.

The doctrine underlying the taxi case, he said, rested upon a "subtle fallacy;" from this fallacy resulted the "unconstitutional assumption" that federal courts possessed the power of "independent judgment" in matters of "general law." The origins of this error lay in the historical conception of the common law as a single "august corpus" found in England and America. "If there were such a transcendental body of law outside of any particular State but obligatory within it unless and until changed by statute," Holmes said, "the Courts of the United States might be right in using their independent judgment as to what it is. But," he confidently pronounced, "there is no such body of law." The pervasive influence of the *Swift* doctrine was to blame for this erroneous conception. Since the doctrine seemed so enmeshed in federal jurisprudence, Holmes would leave it "undisturbed," but he would "not allow it to spread the assumed dominion into new fields." In part Holmes relied on the original draft of section 34 discovered by Charles Warren (probably the nation's leading constitutional historian) which suggested that Story had construed the section contrary to the framer's original intent. But the essentials of his dissent were consistent with views expressed in 1904, 1910, and 1917.[6]

The taxicab opinion roused enormous criticism. Bills were introduced in Congress to end diversity jurisdiction and wipe out *Swift.* Throughout the nation law professors and attorneys took pen in hand to assail the Court in legal journals. Justice Brandeis wrote Felix Frankfurter of Harvard Law School with a proposed draft of legislation aimed at the doctrine and jurisdiction that had made the taxicab company's maneuver possible. Always in close touch with the business of the house and senate judiciary committees and subcommittees, Brandeis indicated to Frankfurter to whom he should send the proposals. Chief Justice William Howard Taft devoted his prestige and influence within the American Bar Association and the Congress to blocking these efforts. He was not immune, however, to the heat of criticism. The chief justice wrote his brother Horace in

June, 1928, in "strictest confidence" that "I shall continue to
be worried by attacks from all academic lawyers who write
college law journals, but I suppose it is not a basis for im-
peachment."[7]

During the decade following the taxicab decision, the
Court drew back from further extensions of the *Swift* doctrine. Charles Evans Hughes, who became Chief Justice in
1930, recalled years later that, "As new cases arose, the conference of judges threshed out the advantages and disadvantages of reverting to the earlier rule. Each time the conviction that the 1842 precedent was wrong seemed to take
firmer root." In 1930 Justice Brandeis wrote a majority
opinion affirming a Missouri State Supreme Court opinion
as binding upon the federal courts. The decision did not,
Brandeis affirmed, offend "constitutional guarantees," despite holdings in *Gelpcke* and *Swift* suggesting the contrary.
Justice George Sutherland in a 1933 majority opinion reversed a lower federal court which had refused to follow
state law as the rule of decision, relying on *Swift* v. *Tyson*.
The next year Benjamin Cardozo for a unanimous Court
summed up the drift of opinions, holding that, despite the
authority deriving from the *Swift* rule, the "*summum jus* of
power . . . will be subordinated . . . to a benign and pru-
dent comity." Even Justice Butler, the author of the taxicab
decision, upheld this position as late as 1937.[8]

Although there were exceptions, these opinions show that
the direction of the Court was away from *Swift* by 1938. But
except for Brandeis' note on "constitutional guarantees,"
these decisions do not reveal a change in thought concerning the theoretical foundation of the concept of general law
or the interpretation of section 34. The cases following the
decision on the taxicab case, unlike the *Muhlker*, *Kuhn* and
Jensen decisions preceding 1928, declined to apply *Swift* simply as a matter of sound policy; they did not enunciate a
jurisprudential theory for refusing to do so. The earlier majority opinions, however, rested upon principles similar to
those stated by Taft, Shiras, and Brewer during the late
nineteenth century. They had come to view *Swift* as a basis

for a federal common law, the development of which was sanctioned by authority implied in Article III of the Constitution. Holmes' dissents were aimed primarily at *this* notion. Holmes had, of course, expressed doubts about *Swift* in his edition of Kent's *Commentaries* of 1873; but it was Meigs, Hare, Pepper, Field, and Miller who developed an analysis of Story's doctrine that paralleled that presented in Justice Holmes' dissents. It was this analysis, articulating as it did a comprehensive jurisprudential theory, rather than the policy-oriented decisions handed down by the Court during the 1930s, that represented the most fundamental challenge to the *Swift* doctrine.[9]

The basis of Holmes' objections was presented in correspondence with Sir Frederick Pollock and Harold J. Laski between 1910 and 1928. To Pollock Holmes wrote that the only source of law in diversity cases was state law, and the voice of the state should be obeyed, "whether it speaks through the legislature or the highest local court." The notion that federal judges could apply an independent judgment as to general law was a "pure usurpation founded upon a subtle fallacy." The idea was traceable to a "very fishy" doctrine of Story, said Holmes, but would have done little harm except for the "influence of . . . some ex-circuit judges [who] . . . have not forgotten the arrogant assumption to which they have been accustomed." In the taxicab case, concluded the Justice, this "arrogant assumption" was pushed to "indefensible lengths in disregarding local decisions."[10]

In letters to Laski, Holmes developed further his views concerning the *Swift* principle. Regarding the notions of his fellow justices concerning the judicial power, Holmes despaired the "tendency to think of judges" as "independent mouthpieces of the infinite." They were in fact, "simply directors of a force that comes from the source that gives them their authority." There was no "mystic overlaw" that federal judges (but no one else) were privy to. The "common law in a state," said Holmes, "is the common law of that state deriving all its authority from the state." The proposition that there existed *"the* common law *in abstracto"* was a "fallacy." In arguing for this position in his dissents, Holmes saw himself as "standing in the ancient ways" in construing the federal judicial power under the Constitution. After his dissent over the decision in the taxi case, the justice wrote Laski that "I will have my whack if I live, if it's my last word."[11]

Holmes and those on the Court who joined him in dissent were not alone in resisting the *Swift* doctrine. We noted that the taxicab case generated several congressional proposals directed at the doctrine and diversity jurisdiction upon which it rested. Proponents of the original Culberson bill had also introduced versions of the original legislation as late as 1910. In 1903 a writer for the *Central Law Journal* urged Congress to deal with *Swift* either by altering the rules of decision act (section 34 of the Judiciary Act of 1789), or if necessary, through constitutional amendment. The writer admitted that the limits of Congressional power over rules of decision were unclear, but if *Swift* "cannot be reached by congressional enactment, is not the 'anomaly' so serious as to call for constitutional amendment?" Ten years later the same author in the same journal argued that diversity jurisdiction had "served its purpose," and that destruction of the *Swift* principle was a major justification for abolishing it.[12]

A major motivation behind these initiatives was a concern for equity. Critics admitted that early in the nineteenth century local uncertainty and prejudice may have justified the formulation of the *Swift* doctrine to carry out the authority implicit in the Constitution's grant of diversity jurisdiction. But by the first third of the twentieth century, these same critics observed, no such justification existed. With "provincialism" no longer a factor, corporations and other non-residents tried cases in federal court solely "to obtain a different interpretation [of law] or to harass adversaries . . . [with the result that federal] jurisdiction is obtained through fraud and perjury." In addition, the availability of diversity jurisdiction and the general law fostered the "evil" of "conflicting law in the same state," a condition that constituted a denial of state sovereignty.[13]

Corporations were a central focus of this reform zeal. Between 1928 and 1932 Senators W. Norris of Nebraska, Thomas J. Walsh of Montana, and others introduced at least eight measures designed to end abuses of the sort practiced in the taxicab case. Norris said in one committee report that it was "becoming more or less common . . . for corporations to be incorporated in one State while they do business in another, and . . . this often occurs simply for the purpose of being able to have the choice of two tribunals in case of litigation." This "forum shopping" discriminated against local businesses which did not have the same privilege; it also was unfair because locals often lacked the resources necessary to carry on protracted appeals all the way to the United States Supreme Court. Finally, this litigation, which could be handled readily by state courts, clogged federal dockets. If corporations and other nonresident litigants were no longer permitted access to federal tribunals on diversity grounds, Norris estimated, a reduction in work load of between 25 and 40 percent would result.[14]

Despite their persistence, Norris and others were largely ineffectual in bringing about changes in federal jurisdiction or the *Swift* doctrine. Lobbyists against the legislative initiatives argued before congressional subcommittees that local suspicion was still a real factor impeding fair consideration of nonresident litigation in state courts. It was admitted that the outright prejudice common during the nineteenth century had generally abated. Instead, defenders of *Swift* and diversity argued, the force of provincialism had become more subtle. Single law firms located in small towns and rural counties were known to have great influence over local judges and juries. The fact that many state judges, from the local level to the supreme court, were elected, further weakened the independence of local courts in trials involving nonresidents, especially corporations. In contrast, federal judges possessed authority that reduced the independence of juries through instructions and other procedures. Too, federal juries were drawn from a much wider area than juries in many local trial courts.[15]

John J. Parker, federal judge of the circuit court of appeals, was quite explicit in expressing these views in an address before a Georgia bar association. He asked members of the bar "if one of you gentlemen were defending a citizen or corporation sued in a rural county in the state of Kentucky or New York, would you prefer to try your case before the local county judge and before a jury composed of the fellow countrymen of the plaintiff, or in the federal court where the judge has jurisdiction over half the state and where the jurors are drawn from a number of counties?" There was but "one answer" to this question, said the judge; any lawyer whose client found himself a litigant in the court of another state would prefer the federal court. The *Swift* doctrine was essential to this process, concluded Parker. It permitted the formulation of a body of uniform rules administered in federal tribunals "upon the basis of which a lawyer can advise his client with assurance as to his rights."[16]

Members of the bar concurred in Parker's views. While still a young attorney for a Montana power and electric company, James W. Moore (future professor of law at Yale Law School) recalled that the *Swift* doctrine, coupled with the right of removal, was vital to the interests of corporations "if the State law was against them." Montana Power was, said Moore, incorporated in Delaware, "with all of its assets in Montana except for a few in Idaho and Wyoming; and it had a tremendous advantage at the time. If it was sued by a citizen of Montana it would just remove . . . they were removing not to get a speedy trial, or anything like that, but to take advantage of *Swift* v. *Tyson*." Robert C. Brown, in a reasoned critique, admitted that diversity and *Swift* created some problems but concluded that the advantages were greater than the disadvantages. "The money lender of the north and east now has . . . a real handicap . . . because of state and sectional prejudice, which, while perhaps dying, is far from dead." Noting the abuses evident in the taxicab case, Brown admitted that federal judges "ought to limit . . . more severely" the *Swift* doctrine, but defended it as essentially valid and useful.[17]

In the face of such arguments, critics often resorted to the Constitution as the basis of their attack on the *Swift* principle. In doing so, they appealed to Holmes' dissents, emphasizing as they did the "subtle fallacy," of the notion that the common law was a "brooding omnipresence in the sky," upon which rested the federal courts' "unconstitutional assumption of power." Raymond T. Johnson in the *Kentucky Law Journal* of 1929 summed up the views held by many. The doctrine of *Swift* v. *Tyson* was a "violation of the Diverse Citizenship Clause of the Constitution and is therefore an unconstitutional assumption of power." Besides this "most basic approach" to the controversy, Johnson pointed out further that the doctrine was contrary to the "principle of comity" and was "predicated upon a misconception of . . . [section 34] and is therefore violative of its true intendment." The author hoped that a change in the membership of the Supreme Court would "bring [the Court's authority] in line with the spirit of the constitutional provision and the letter of" the thirty-fourth section.[18]

Thomas W. Shelton in the *Virginia Law Review* of 1928 and Armistead M. Dobie in the same journal of 1930 reiterated similar conclusions. Shelton contended that the Court's application of *Swift* asserted power over substantive rules of law that Congress did not possess. More reserved, Dobie admitted that congressional authority over the matter was open to question, but he did agree with both Shelton and Johnson that the only real hope for removing *Swift* lay with the Supreme Court. "The Supreme Court might yet . . . definitely and expressly overrule *Swift* v. *Tyson*," he concluded. "This appears, in the light of the willingness of the present Supreme Court to reverse previous decisions believed to be erroneous . . . to present a larger measure of hope than any of the other suggested remedies."[19]

The research of Charles Warren, another attorney concerned about the implications of the *Swift* doctrine, provided further evidence for criticizing the 1842 opinion. A major assumption shared by most critics of Story's decision was that it violated the true intent of the framers of section 34. Warren, while assistant attorney general under President Woodrow Wilson, discovered the original drafts of the section. As we have seen, the final version read "That the laws of the several states . . . shall be regarded as rules of decision . . . in cases where they apply." Story had construed the word *laws* to exclude the general commercial law, though he affirmed that federal judges were bound to follow state statutes, local customs, and state judicial constructions of these. The original draft discovered by Warren stated that "the Statutue law of the several states in force for the time being and their unwritten and common law now in use, whether by adoption from the common law of England, the ancient statutes of the same, or otherwise." Comparing the two versions, Warren concluded that the more concise laws of the final version was simply a stylistic summary of the longer original. Because the original seemed to give a more detailed listing of the local law binding upon federal judges, Warren concluded that Story had been wrong in excluding the so-called "general commercial law" from the phrase "laws."[20]

Warren's scholarship became a standard link in the chain of reasoning directed against *Swift*. Holmes cited it in the taxicab case, as did Johnson and other writers of law review articles. But even as adamant a critic of *Swift* v. *Tyson* as Felix Frankfurter (whose views will be discussed shortly) admitted privately that he did not consider Warren's discovery as the "last word on the subject." A careful comparison of the draft and original suggests another interpretation of the change from the longer to the shorter version. As William Crosskey many years later would show, the draft included the phrases "now in use" and "for the time being," strongly implying that the framers were thinking about the law in force in 1789 (the year in which the statute was written). The final version, however, had no such qualifying language. Warren had said that this was simply a stylistic change; but Crosskey pointed out that the change implied an alteration of intent on the part of the framers of the statute. He argued further that the phrase "where they apply" in section 34, admitted that there *were* cases in which federal judges were not bound to follow local law, as Story had said. In addition, Crosskey pointed out that during the early nineteenth century the concept of general commercial law was a widely shared jurisprudential assumption that was consistent with accepted conflict-of-law theory.[21]

The inconclusiveness of Warren's discovery reflected the bar's general inability to agree upon the value or legitimacy of the *Swift* principle during the first third of the twentieth century. A similar lack of agreement pervaded the nation's law schools. Among the most influential law professors whose teaching focused on *Swift* was Joseph Henry Beale of Harvard. Beale encountered the notion of general law in Thayer's constitutional law class as a student in 1886. In 1891 he joined the Harvard faculty and during a long and distinguished career had a profound impact on the nation's legal education in several areas. He was the first dean of the University of Chicago School of Law, president of the Association of American Law Schools, and cofounder of the American Law Institute in 1922. His most significant impact, however, was in the academic study of conflict of laws. When Beale first became interested in the subject in the late 1890s, its standing as a body of law was far from clear. By the 1920s, Beale's publications and teaching had been largely responsible for bringing the field into academic respectability and importance. Beale became the first reporter of the restatement of conflicts for the American Law Institute, published the leading case book in the field, and trained many of the first teachers of the subject. Although his ideas were eventually repudiated by even his own students, they continued to be influential through the 1940s and beyond.[22]

Beale's major—perhaps overriding—goal was the establishment of predictability and certainty in law. He was aware that the federal system of the United States fostered legal diversity, making uniformity virtually impossible. But Beale firmly believed that a "single centralized government," although having the means to create uniformity, was too high a price to pay for certainty. "Wisely," he said in 1917, Americans "have clung to . . . local laws; laws that we know, that are made by ourselves, that serve our local needs, are best." Beale was convinced that an examination of the "irreducible minimum of peculiar local laws" would reveal that "they rest on some special local need, some peculiarity of place, people, history, experience." Beyond this law was the embodiment of a peoples' "idea of right"; it was neither "historical accident" nor "subtle metaphysic," but was "a tool, with which society works out its activities." The Harvard professor considered himself part of a "small but important" school of legal thinkers who applied the "historical method" of "observation and induction" in order to scientifically determine for "the first time since the world began" an "intelligent statement of the principles of law."[23]

These general philosophical assumptions were back of Beale's basic principle of conflict-of-law theory—the idea of territoriality. According to the principle of territoriality there could be but one law ruling in any sovereign jurisdiction. This law had no operation outside the limits of the sovereign's authority, and the law of no other sovereign had effect within this territorial jurisdiction. In his classes on conflicts, which became a "conspicuous feature" of the third-year curriculum of Harvard Law School, Beale used *Swift* v. *Tyson* as a foil for his theory of territoriality. Student notebooks from the years 1900 to 1930—including those of such distinguished members of the legal profession as Felix Frankfurter, Robert Leflar, David Cavers, Manley O. Hudson, Zechariah Chafee, Thomas Reed Powell—reveal this process.[24]

Because there was only one law of the sovereign, which depended upon the "ideas and minds of people" living within its juridiction, the conception of a federal common law different and distinct from the local laws was "erroneous." Federal courts were in fact, said Beale, empowered

only to administer the law of the state. The fact that state
and federal judges "may differ cannot mean that there are
two laws in the jurisdiction," the professor told his students,
"but merely that one court or both is mistaken in its statement or interpretation of the law." In class, following the
format of his casebook, Beale asked students to compare
Shiras' Murry Railroad opinion with Grosscup's Pennsylvania Railroad decision (discussed above). The notebooks
show that Beale accepted Grosscup's denial of general law,
whereas Shiras was, the professor observed, "erroneous in
saying that there was a U.S. common law." Beale conceded
that Congress could change the local law through legislation, but until it did so the "old common law remained in
force." He admitted further that state courts did not always
decide like cases in the same way; this meant that one of the
lawyer's most important functions was to decide when the
decisions of "his state do not represent the law of his state."
Because the *Swift* doctrine contributed further to this confusion, it was all the more objectionable.[25]

In his seminar Beale developed other reasons for criticizing the theory underlying *Swift* v. *Tyson*. The notion of general law harkened back, he said, to an eighteenth- and early
nineteenth-century theory of conflict of laws holding that
"international law has international application because
there is a mass of internationally accepted customs." This
theory was prevalent in continental jurisprudence, and was
antithetical to the common-law emphasis on territoriality.
Story's treatise on conflicts had "mixed" all theories "without discrimination," perhaps because he had written it hur-
riedly in one year. In order to reconcile the theories of territoriality and internationality of "accepted customs," Story
used the idea of comity, which (as we have seen) provided
a jurisprudential justification for courts' application of international law, while accepting the supremacy of local law
in principle. Although Beale acknowledged that Story's
ideas had been useful, he declared them "outdated." They
represented, he said, a "survival" of eighteenth century
"natural law" assumptions which scholars of the "analytical

and historical school" had been fighting for two generations.[26]

John Chipman Gray was another influential Harvard Law School scholar who criticized *Swift.* As early as 1892 in an article published in the *Harvard Law Review,* Gray defined the legal process as the "science of actual, or positive law," according to which courts decided real cases. His primary concern was the nature and sources of law "now," rather than how law had developed to reach its present form. In 1909 Gray published a book that treated more fully these and related themes. In several places he castigated the *Swift* doctrine as an "anomaly" which was "inconsistent" with any "scientific" theory of law. Gray linked *Swift* with the Court's "singularly feeble" decision in *Gelpcke,* contrasting it with the "masterly" dissent of Justice Miller.[27]

Although the professor admitted that the language of section 34 was ambiguous as to rules of decision, he rejected the concept of general law as totally invalid. The federal and state courts derived their "political authority" from different sovereigns. While Congress could, admitted Gray, establish rules of decision for federal courts, until it had done so the only law federal judges were empowered to apply was state law. Ignoring the fact that the Court deciding *Swift* was unanimous and predominantly Jacksonian Democrat, Gray blamed the "anomalous" opinion on Story, who was, he said, fond of "glittering generalities," and "possessed by a restless vanity." As we have seen, Justice Holmes cited Gray's views in his *Kuhn* dissent of 1910, and repeated the professor's opinion of Story in letters to Pollock and Laski. Gray's ideas gained a still wider audience when he took over the teaching of Thayer's class on constitutional law at Harvard in 1904.[28]

Beale and Gray based their criticism of *Swift* on grounds of legal theory. Felix Frankfurter, another professor of law at Harvard, approached the issue from a different perspective. To Frankfurter (who had coauthored a major study of the administration and business at the Supreme Court) *Swift* raised issues that were essentially those of "administrative effectiveness and procedural adaptations—matters not of principle but wise expediency." In his teaching and publication, Frankfurter reiterated the standard objections to *Swift,* linking them to a basic dissatisfaction with diversity jurisdiction in general. Diversity and *Swift* fostered, he said, "elements of unfairness," a "double system of laws" in the same state which was "plainly hostile to the reign of law," gave corporations an unfair advantage, burdened federal dockets with cases that could just as easily be disposed of in state courts, and undermined the collegiality of federal judges by creating the necessity for too many of them. A strong proponent of abolishing diversity, Frankfurter argued that Congress should take the first step in this direction by enacting legislation. Whether the "roots of the doctrine be in rational theory or obscure impulse, it is now too strongly imbedded in our law for judicial self-correction," he said. "Legislation should remove this doctrine, which, though derived from diverse citizenship jurisdiction, denies its basis."[29]

Frankfurter encountered *Swift* as a student in Beale's conflict-of-laws class in 1900. A quarter of a century later he criticized the doctrine in his own classes on federal jurisdiction. His seminars produced many theses, some of which chose as their topic the issues raised by *Swift* and diversity jurisdiction. Like other lawyers of his time, Frankfurter was appalled by the taxicab decision of 1928. He wrote Holmes that he considered the justice's dissent the term's "masterpiece." In his teaching, Frankfurter was critical of the decision and the theory underlying *Swift* v. *Tyson.* Although he admitted that the doctrine was probably consistent with notions of law prevalent in Story's time, he argued that according to accepted principles of twentieth-century jurisprudence, courts did not "make law" but "applied it," a tenet which *Swift* violated. In addition, he told classes, the *Swift* doctrine generated confusion as to the local law. Frankfurter believed that Congress possessed the power to codify substantive rules of law but did not view the prospect with enthusiasm. These and other ideas the professor im-

parted to students, who would later make important contributions of their own to American law.[30]

But the views of the Harvard scholars did not go unchal-
lenged by other teachers of law in the nation's universities.
Frederick Green of the University of Illinois School of Law
critized Gray's analysis of *Swift.* "The Supreme Court has
power to secure uniform and desirable rules of decision in
federal courts throughout the Union," he said in 1924,
"and, at the cost of conflicting rules in particular states, to
dispense the same justice to the parties whatever the district
in which their case happens to arise." Hessel E. Yntema and
George H. Jaffin, who were associated with the University
of Pennsylvania School of Law, published a searching statistical and analytical study of diversity jurisdiction and *Swift*
in 1931. Their findings refuted Frankfurter's argument on
virtually every point. Other articles addressed the contention, developed in Beale's courses and elsewhere, that there
was no jurisprudential justification for a federal common
law.[31]

Arthur L. Corbin, professor of law at Yale University,
gave perhaps the most significant reply to the Harvard professors. Like Beale, Corbin was committed to a systematic
ordering of legal rules through restatements and other devices. But his views as to the ultimate source of and authority behind law differed from Beale's. For Corbin there was
no "universal and unchangeable rule" of law. The common
law applied in English and American courts was founded
upon no "great body of already crystalized rules . . . [or
even] a set of extremely broad principles." This common
law was, said Corbin, a system growing over centuries "con-
structed by hundreds of thousands of decisions in actual
cases." The Yale professor exclaimed that there was a high
degree of uniformity and consistency discernable throughout these cases, if one took the time to study them all. This
fact made it possible to predict certain results in litigation,
giving lawyers the means to make their living. In this "fundamental aspect" Corbin observed, the common law was
"no different" from the laws "we think we have discovered

in physics or in chemistry;" they needed periodic reappraisal and restatement in "light of wider observation and
more clearly correct analysis."[32]

Corbin applied these ideas in his consideration of the
Swift doctrine. Commenting upon Holmes' dissent in the
taxicab case, the law professor acknowledged that there was,
strictly speaking, no *federal* common law distinct from the
law of the state, as Holmes had said. But Corbin did not
accept Holmes' reasoning that only local law provided rules
of decision in federal court. Federal judges, he said, were
"fully authorized to declare and build up common law in
the cases properly before them" like the judges in state
courts. Although "added conflict" might result, this was
"nothing new in either kind or quality." A legal rule, Corbin
stressed, must "fight for its life, whether the rule is enunciated by a state court or the United States Supreme
Court."[33]

When the Supreme Court developed the common law
"with respect to men and events" within a state, there was,
said Corbin using Holmes' famous phraseology, "definite
authority behind it" and no "unconstitutional assumption of
power." The federal courts were operating no differently
than the state courts in such matters. Differences in doctrine evidenced in state and federal tribunals contributed to
a "healthy variation . . . based upon new experience,
changing conditions, and new customs and desires." For
Corbin, the fundamental character of the common law did
not rest upon a "substratum of grand eternal principles"; it
was rather a process whereby "judicial decisions and administrative action should continually be readjusted to the
needs and desires of mankind." Proceeding from this assumption, Corbin implied that small harm and no little
good had resulted from the *Swift* doctrine.[34]

Given the scope of legislative initiatives in Congress, debate in legal periodicals, and disagreement among academ-
ics in the nation's leading law schools, controversy involving
the *Swift* doctrine may be considered a significant political
and legal issue of the day. This was so in part because the

Swift principle raised challenging questions concerning the proper balance between federal and state government and the limits of federal judicial discretionary authority in maintaining that balance. But as had been true during the late nineteenth century, enmeshed with these issues of federalism were other factors that created further complications.

J. B. Fordham pointed out in 1929 that diversity jurisdiction and the *Swift* doctrine threatened small-scale local business because they gave unfair advantage to large corporations. Justice Harlan F. Stone wrote Holmes regarding the taxicab decision in 1928, "It really seems shocking that we should allow our jurisdiction to be used to set aside a well settled local policy like this." Behind such practical considerations were more general but nonetheless significant philosophical presumptions shared by many Americans during the period. Professor Beale, as noted above, argued that local customs reflected important social values which were too important to be swallowed up by a central government. Louis D. Brandeis was among the most famous proponents of this sort of localism. "Local customs, traditions, and the peculiar habits of mind of . . . [a state's] people have resulted in a spirit which is its own," he said. "This is manifest partly in its statutes, but even more largely in what may be termed its common law." More directly to the point, Brandeis held that "the present tendency [in the United States] towards centralization must be arrested, if we are to attain the American ideals, and that for it must be substituted intense development of life through activities in the several states and localities." Faithful to these assumptions, Brandeis opposed implementation of the Federal Rules of Civil Procedure because they would supersede distinctive local practices.[35]

Another basis for resistance to *Swift* grew out of tensions associated with the public's distrust of law and the legal profession. Elihu Root expressed the fears of many members of the legal profession in 1912: "aggravation of the growing contempt for the whole institution of law . . . which if not abated by intelligent and scientific reform will inevitably bring disaster to our whole social and political fabric." Reiterating a theme familiar during the late nineteenth century, another prominent attorney pointed out that too many lawyers "sold their talents to corporations" and remained "like a sordid fringe to the judicial garment." In order that the legal profession "regain its ancient place of equal nobility with the ministry and the medical profession," he continued, "lawyers must demonstrate that, above . . . pecuniary gain" they also "cherish the ideal of service-ableness to mankind." [36]

Because the *Swift* doctrine permitted lawyers to employ "elaborate learning" to gain advantages for corporate and other nonresident clients, it was one ingredient contributing to the public's suspicion of law and the legal profession. Judge Charles I. Dawson expressed this view in an article on the doctrine in 1931. American citizens "cannot understand why the law should be one thing in a state court and something else in the Federal Court," he said. "In this day and time, when it is the fashion to belittle the law and its administration in courts of justice, it should be a matter of vital concern to members of the [legal] profession" that this conflict exists. As early as 1914 Louis D. Brandeis, Roscoe Pound and others expressed similar concerns in a report on *Efficiency in the Administration of Justice*. [37]

The changing character of American jurisprudential thinking was another factor implicit in the debate over the *Swift* doctrine. During the late nineteenth century, assumptions underlying the conception of law as universal, were undermined by an increased emphasis on sovereignty and territoriality as the ultimate basis of legal principle. Despite the innumerable cases handed down by courts daily, scientific analysis of the historical evolution of doctrine could bring to light, as Christiphor C. Langdell had said, a comparatively few fundamental principles of law. During the first third of the twentieth century, a legal positivism associated with the work of Oliver Wendell Holmes increasingly came to dominate American legal thought. In 1880 in his classic *The Common Law* Holmes stated that experience not

logic had been the real "life of the law." This eventually
famous proposition reflected Holmes's conviction that social
conditions and conscious and unconscious human impul-
ses—shaped by history—were the main forces at work in the
development of law. According to this perception, law was
neither the expression of universal principle nor even primarily a logical structure; it was ultimately the manifestation of the lawmaker's opinion as to what was socially necessary and expedient.[38]

Holmes's conception of law was not widely accepted until
after the turn of the century when it became a central
theme of legal theories developed in the nation's law schools
and courts. Gray, Frankfurter, Corbin, and most of the
other critics and defenders of the *Swift* doctrine applied in
their arguments assumptions consistent with legal positivism. Like Holmes himself, Gray emphasized that courts
made law, but should do so in deference to the legislature.
Frankfurter's call for efficient judicial administration and
expeditious legislative reform reflected an awareness of the
constructive or negative economic and social impact of
court decisions. Corbin's insistence on continual reshaping
of common-law rules to changing society acknowledged further the need to perceive the origin and function of legal
rules as part of a broader social milieu. Thus, as had been
the case with the historical and analytical jurists in the late
nineteenth century, the dominant mode of legal thinking
after 1900 provided both supporters and opponents of *Swift*
jurisprudential tools with which to maintain their position.
This suggests that, like the debate in Congress, division on
the Supreme Court, and disagreement among members of
the bar and teachers of law, the legal thought of the period
was at an impasse concerning the *Swift* doctrine. Something
had to be done, but what?[39]

THE FACTS, TRIAL, AND DECISION OF ERIE

Hughestown Pennsylvania was a village of 2800 people in
1934. One warm, moonless July night some time after two

A.M., an unemployed worker named Harry James Tompkins, 27 years old, walked home along the railroad tracks that ran through Hughestown. Months before, Tompkins had been laid off from the Pittson Stove Works. Since then he had supported himself, infant daughter, and wife by working various odd jobs. On the night of July 26 Tompkins had visited his mother-in-law, where he had stayed until after midnight. Friends had given him a ride to a street corner near the tracks; his home was down the rails, not far away. Alongside the road bed was a well-worn footpath that Tompkins had taken often. He did not leave the path when he heard the whistle and saw the light of a train coming from the opposite direction. It was a train of the Erie Railroad.[40]

As the engine and cars rumbled by, Tompkins neared a cross path that intersected the tracks, where he intended to turn toward home. But he never made it. Just as he reached the intersecting path, "something" protruding from the train smashed into him. Shortly afterward a neighbor of Tompkins was awakened by someone in the street shouting that there had been an accident. The neighbor went out into the night and found Tompkins laying unconscious near the rails with his severed right arm nearby. The young man was taken to the hospital where the stump of his arm was amputated. He recovered quickly, and went looking for a lawyer.

It happened that a shirt manufacturer in the Hughestown area heard about the accident and the need for an attorney. The son of the businessman was Bernard G. Nemeroff, 27 years old, who practiced law in New York City. Nemeroff's partner was Bernard Kaufman, also 27. Their office was rented from an older lawyer, who had working for him a 21-year-old attorney named Aaron L. Danzig. Nemeroff had been practicing law for five years since his graduation from the part-time division of the New York University law school in 1929, but his business had not been great. When his father recommended his son to Tompkins, Nemeroff did not hesitate in taking the case. He asked Kaufman and Danzig to help him do the research.

Their research revealed that the case raised a central question: 'What duty (if any) did the railroad owe to travelers to guard against the sort of carelessness that had contributed to Tompkins' injury? The attorneys found in the Pennsylvania law an unencouraging answer to this question. The Pennsylvania state cases held that travelers on a path running parallel to railroad tracks were regarded as trespassers to whom the railroad owed no duty except to avoid "wanton negligence." By contrast, travelers on a cross path were considered "licensees," which meant simply that the railroad was bound by law to take at least "ordinary care" to avoid injuring them. There were older opinions that imposed on the railroad liability for travelers in both situations, but the *Falchetti* decision of the Pennsylvania Supreme Court in 1934 overruled these cases, holding that those in Tompkins' position were trespassers. Tompkins could not prove "wanton negligence," Nemeroff and his colleagues knew. Thus suit in Pennsylvania would mean disaster.[41]

But there were alternatives. The Erie Railroad was a New York corporation and Tompkins was a resident of Pennsylvania. Also, the damages for the injury were greater than $3000. The diversity of residence and the amount in controversy qualified the litigation for entry in the federal district court. The question then arose, however, whether state law bound federal courts in such cases. After further research, the three attorneys discovered section 34 of the Judiciary Act of 1789 and its construction by Joseph Story in the case of *Swift* v. *Tyson*. According to Story's interpretation of the statute, federal judges applied their own judgment as to the general law. In accident cases of the sort involving Tompkins, most states had adopted the liberal rule given in the Restatements of Torts, making railroads liable for injuries caused by negligence occuring to travelers on both parallel and intersecting paths. Nemeroff and his colleagues reasoned that the restatement rule would govern Tompkins' case if they could show that under the *Swift* doctrine Pennsylvania law was not controlling. It turned out, however, that the Federal District Court of Pennsylvania had chosen to adhere to the local law. The attorneys then decided to initiate the suit against the Erie Railroad in the United States District Court for the Southern District of New York on August 29, 1934.[42]

The New York City firm of Davis, Polk, Wardell, Gardiner, and Reed represented the Erie Railroad Company. The firm's senior partner was a former United States ambassador to Great Britain and unsuccessful presidential candidate, John W. Davis; its chief trial lawyer was Theodore Kiendl. In 1934 Kiendl was 44 years old, a graduate of Columbia College and of Columbia Law School. Upon researching the case, Kiendl found that the Pennsylvania law best served the interests of his client; he also realized that the *Swift* doctrine put into question whether the federal court would apply the local law. But further research revealed that the *Swift* doctrine had had a rather complex and at times "scandalous" record (noting the taxicab opinion), and that in several cases since 1930 the Supreme Court had shown less willingness to apply the venerable precedent. Kiendl perceived that in an appeal he could argue to limit or perhaps overrule the *Swift* principle. To make such an appeal, however, it was first necessary to try the case before the federal judge and a jury.

Tompkins' complaint argued that he had been walking on a footpath running parallel to the railroad bed when a "black" projection from a moving train struck him. The accident caused the loss of his right arm and was due to the negligence of the railroad. Damages amounted to $100,000. In its answer, the Erie denied the claim, arguing that Tompkins' own carelessness had contributed to the accident, therefore offsetting any fault of the railroad. By the summer of 1936 a lengthy record was prepared, including the testimony of those involved and various photographs of the place of the accident, and the case went to trial before Federal District Judge Samuel Mandelbaum.

Mandelbaum had been a colorful "people's lawyer" in the lower east side of New York City before election to the assembly and then state senate as a member of the Tammany organization. The politician's "devotion . . . humility . . . self-effacing kindness endeared him to his colleagues, urban and upstate, Republican and Democrat."[43] Mandelbaum was a close friend of Mr. and Mrs. Franklin D. Roosevelt; by 1932 he had become an important power in the New York Democratic party. In 1936 Congress created several new judgeships in the Southern District of New York; President Roosevelt nominated his friend to fill one of them. Despite opposition from the state bar and the press (who denounced "judicial spoils"), the United States Senate, responding to a flood of letters praising the nominee's character, confirmed the loyal Democrat. *Erie Railroad* v. *Tompkins* was Mandelbaum's first civil case.[44]

The trial started on October 5, 1936 and lasted four days. Nemeroff retained Everett G. Hunt, an experienced and "very successful" negligence lawyer. "Stubby" Hunt had tried numerous cases similar to Tompkins' and had cultivated an ability to generate sympathy for his clients among jurors. Hunt and Kiendl were friends; during the trial the friendly adversaries followed quite different strategies. Kiendl was organized and cool in argument, whereas Hunt appeared disorganized, while displaying the skills of an actor before the jury, exploiting weaknesses in the railroad's defense.

"Something," like an opened door, protruding from the train had crushed the plaintiff to the ground, said Hunt, and the impact had forced his client to the ground, thrusting his arm under the wheels of the passing train, severing it clean. When Kiendl tried to argue that the train had been inspected shortly before the accident, Hunt produced testimony from the railroad's inspector that he could not remember exactly whether he had looked at the particular car allegedly responsible for Tompkins' injury. Following several other such tactical victories, Hunt concluded by pointing out to the jury that the residents of Hughestown had used the parallel path for years without objection from the Erie Railroad, justifying Tompkins' confidence in using the route on the night of the accident. His client's medical bill amounted to $449.00; before the loss of his arm Tompkins had been earning between $21.00 and $28.00 a week, and was now unable to work. With this, Hunt rested his case.

Kiendl moved for a dismissal. "I want to call you Honor's attention to the fact [that] this permissive pathway doctrine [the liberal rule given in Restatement of Torts] is not applicable in this case under the decisions of the highest courts of Pennsylvania."[45] Here the railroad's attorney attempted to bring in the argument that Pennsylvania local law should govern the case, but Mandelbaum rejected the effort and denied the motion for dismissal. Kiendl then made his defense, which relied heavily on the testimony of the yard inspector on duty during the night of the argument. As we have seen, Hunt successfully challenged this testimony and Kiendl was left with the contention that Tompkins may have lost his footing, causing him to fall. Hunt pointed out that Tompkins had "walked the route plenty of times," casting doubt on this tenuous theory as well. Finally, both sides rested. In his summation, Kiendl asked Mandelbaum to instruct the jury that the plaintiff had failed to prove "wanton negligence," the principle embodied in the Pennsylvania law. The judge refused and Kiendl excepted.

On October 13, 1936 Judge Mandelbaum charged the jury that Tompkins was bound to prove the railroad's negligence, following the liberal rule given in the restatement. The jury retired, deliberated, and returned a verdict for Tompkins amounting to $30,000. Kiendl asked that the verdict be set aside, a motion which Mandelbaum denied. The clerk of the court entered the judgment, the total, including interests and costs, amounting to $30,260.

But Tompkins did not get his money. The Erie Railroad appealed to the United States Circuit Court for the Second Circuit. Shortly before the appeal an employee of the railroad contacted someone who knew Tompkins, informing him that the railroad was ready to settle the case for $7500. Tompkins was willing, but when he discussed the offer with Nemeroff, the attorney invited him to his home in Baldwin, New York, in order to remove his client from temptation.

After two weeks, during which time the appeal had begun, Tompkins returned to Pennsylvania, to wait.

The appeal raised 18 assignments of error, but the tenth was the most important: "The Court erred in failing to hold at the conclusion of the plaintiff's case that the permissive pathway doctrine did not apply to longitudinal pathways such as herein involved, under the laws of the State of Pennsylvania."[46] Kiendl's brief developed an argument challenging this and the other "errors" occurring at trial, concluding that the law of Pennsylvania should apply because "the highest courts of that state have completely established a settled policy regarding local matters."[47] Perhaps because he had not yet decided how to deal with *Swift*, Kiendl did not cite the decision in his brief.

The brief of Nemeroff and Hunt responded point by point to Kiendl's challenges. Regarding the central issue of the federal court's obligation to follow Pennsylvania doctrine, Tompkins' counsel stated that federal judges were free to exercise an "independent judgment whenever the law of the place is contrary to a general common law."[48] The appeal was heard by a panel consisting of Learned Hand, Martin Manton, and Thomas Swan. On June 7, 1936 Swan delivered the circuit court's decision: "Upon questions of general law the federal courts are free, in the absence of a local statute, to exercise their independent judgment as to what the law is; and it is well settled that the question of the responsibility of a railroad for injuries caused by its servants is one of general law." Swan did not cite *Swift* v. *Tyson*, but more on point, gave Justice Brewer's *Baugh* opinion of 1892, as precedent.[49]

The decision did not show, however, that Hand and Swan were troubled by the Erie case. During and after the argument of the appeal, the two judges discussed at length the advisability of extending the *Swift* doctrine in yet another opinion. They were sensitive to the sort of criticism raised against the federal judiciary following the decision in the taxicab case, which continued to cast a shadow eight years afters its decision. Hand and Swan appreciated the flexibility that the *Swift* doctrine gave federal judges, especially where state law was obscure or (to their minds) unfair; but they were also concerned about potential abuse arising from an unwise use of discretionary authority. Finally, the judges agreed to apply the well-established doctrine of *Swift* v. *Tyson,* and decided the case accordingly.[50]

Unfortunately for Tompkins, the circuit court's decision did not bring recovery. The Erie Railroad was prepared to make a final appeal to the United States Supreme Court. Now that the circuit court had decided the case, only a stay from one of the Supreme Court justices, or the Court itself, could postpone further the railroad paying Tompkins. It was July and the Supreme Court was in summer recess. Kiendl had no choice but to go to Justice Benjamin Cardozo of New York, to request the stay. Cardozo granted an appointment to Kiendl and Tompkins' attorneys Nemeroff, Danzig, and Fred Rees (Hunt's partner) to present their respective arguments concerning the matter. The Supreme Court had not taken a negligence case for some time, and Rees felt that they were not likely to do so in this instance.

Rees failed to consider, however, that the Court had been backing off from *Swift* since 1930; Cardozo, in fact, had written one such decision in 1933. Kiendl told the justice that if he denied the stay his client would pursue the appeal no further. Perhaps Cardozo saw in the *Erie* case an opportunity for the whole Court to face squarely the questions raised by the concept of general law. While recent cases had presented these issues peripherally, *Erie* raised them directly. Also, the Court had been for several years boldly challenging the constitutionality of New Deal legislation. Given these considerations, it may have seemed appropriate to face a problem that had troubled the nation's courts and legal profession for nearly three-quarters of a century. Whatever the reasons, Cardozo granted the stay, the case moved on to the Supreme Court, and Tompkins was again left waiting for his money.[51]

The appeal was filed on August 30, 1937. It stated essentially that the trial court had erred in refusing to apply

Pennsylvania law. William Claytor (who had been Judge
Hand's law clerk the year before when *Erie* was heard in the
circuit court) told Justice Brandeis, whom he now served,
that *Erie Railroad* v. *Tompkins* was "just another" diversity
case. The clerk to Chief Justice Charles Evans Hughes expressed similar views. Evidently, however, the members of
the Court saw something more in the case; the petition for
certiorari was granted on October 11, 1937.[52]

The briefs focused on the issue of general law. Kiendl
maintained that the Pennsylvania Supreme Court's *Falchetti*
decision (holding that travelers in Tompkins' position were
trespassers) established the rule that should have been given
to the jury. The railroad's attorney dealt skillfully with the
Swift doctrine. He argued that the precedents following the
decision in 1842 held that federal judges would follow the
local law when it "established the rule of law with sufficient
definiteness and finality to constitute it a local rule of property, action, or conduct." As we have seen, this summed up
precisely the way in which federal courts had explained
their development of the *Swift* doctrine. Years later Kiendl
recollected that he chose this strategy, rather than arguing
for an overrule of *Swift*, because he was "convinced that a
head on attack might be fatal." The attorney also maintained that Tompkins had been "grossly careless" and "con-
tributorily negligent," thus relieving the railroad of any responsibility for the accident.[53] In reply, Tompkins' counsel
held that the jury had been correctly charged according to
the general law.

Erie Railroad v. *Tompkins* was argued on Monday, January
31, 1938. Kiendl and Rees made their arguments before a
Court including Chief Justice Hughes, Louis D. Brandeis,
James C. McReynolds, Harlan F. Stone, Pierce Butler,
Owen J. Roberts, Hugo L. Black, and Stanley Reed. The
day of the *Erie* argument was Justice Reed's first on the
Court; Justice Black had been appointed only a short time
before. Benjamin Cardozo was not present. Kiendl recollected that his presentation "had not proceeded very far before Mr. Justice Brandeis pointedly inquired about our

views with regard to the *Swift* v. *Tyson* case." Kiendl responded that he viewed the doctrine as "unfortunate in its consequences but that nevertheless, its acceptance by so many courts for so many years precluded . . . suggesting that the doctrine be overruled." Following this statement "practically all the members of the Court then participated in a discussion of *Swift* v. *Tyson*," and a "large part" of Kiendl's argument "revolved around it." Apparently the standing of the *Swift* doctrine was the key issue as far as the Court was concerned, even though the attorneys for neither side had raised the question in their presentation.[54]

Shortly afterward, probably the following Saturday, February 5, the justices met in conference to discuss *Erie* (and other cases). Chief Justice Hughes announced that, "If we wish to overrule *Swift* v. *Tyson*, here is our opportunity." Butler and McReynolds did not agree. They accepted Kiendl's contention that Tompkins, not the railroad, had been negligent and stood by the traditional rule that such questions were governed by the general law. Reed and Black favored overruling *Swift*, but were concerned that in doing so the Court would foreclose Tompkins recovering his judgment. Stone, Roberts, and Brandeis joined Hughes in emphasizing the need to dispose of the old precedent. Finally, the chief justice (no doubt aware of his colleague's long-time resistance to the doctrine as evidenced by concurrence in Holmes' dissents) assigned the writing of the opinion to Brandeis.[55]

Aside from agreeing to overrule *Swift*, the justices had not apparently decided upon the form or content of the *Erie* decision. Sometime before February 11 Stone wrote Black concerning another opinion, commented that the "basis of our decision in the Pennsylvania railroad accident case is that we follow local law when it is well enough defined so that we know what it is." This suggests that for Stone, and probably the rest of the concurring majority, the focus of the *Erie* decision was the local law, and little else.[56]

By February 28, Brandeis began to draft his opinion. It was the justice's practice to write out drafts in longhand, using the Court's overnight printing service to prepare a smooth printed form from which to work the following morning. The process could, and usually did, go through numerous drafts before an opinion was in satisfactory form to circulate among the other members of the Court. Sometimes Brandeis discussed decisions with his clerk, though in *Erie* he worked primarily alone. The justice did assign his clerk, William Claytor, to research the status of Pennsylvania law in order to determine whether, according to the local precedents, there might be some means for Tompkins' recovery if the case was retried. By the October term of 1937 Chief Justice Hughes had given Brandeis a reduced work load (he was nearly 82 years old), so he was able to devote a good deal of time to preparing the opinion.[57]

Brandeis' handwritten and printed drafts, notes, and memoranda included in the file of the case, reveal the process, sources, and thinking that resulted in the final opinion. The earliest drafts were dated February 28, and subsequent numbers indicate that the justice was aiming for Monday, March 28 as the probable date for the reading of the decision. During the month he must prepare the opinion, circulate it among his colleagues for comment, and then incorporate or at least answer these comments in the eventual decision. The first printed drafts give a succinct summary of the facts, leading to the issues raised by the case. "The only matters requiring consideration are the alleged Pennsylvania law and whether it should govern cases tried in the federal courts," concluded this printed draft.[58]

Handwritten notes, however, reveal that Brandeis intended to develop a more comprehensive decision. These show clearly his sources and emerging argument. Brandeis cited the article by Johnson in the *Kentucky Law Journal* of 1929 concerning the constitutional issues involving *Swift*. Other articles and treatises include Gray's *Nature and Sources of Law*, Thayer's article on *Gelpcke*, Pepper's *Borderland of State and Federal Law*, Holmes' dissents in *Kuhn*, and the taxicab case, and Hare's *Constitutional Law*. Phrases referring to the "unconstitutionality" of *Swift* v. *Tyson*, and comments concerning the "unfairness" and lack of uniformity in local law are noted several times. Further statements declare that the *Swift* doctrine "rests upon [a] misunderstanding" of section 34 and a "violation of [the] diversity of citizenship clause" of the Constitution. To a large degree the notes at this stage summarize Johnson's article, the views of the leading late-nineteenth-century critics of *Swift,* and Holmes' dissent.[59]

As Brandeis gathered his citations and fashioned his arguments, Claytor put together a lengthy memoranda on the Pennsylvania law. "I think that in Pennsylvania it must be now taken as settled," the young man wrote, "that the *Falchetti* case determines the liability of travelers" in Tompkins' position. It was true, he pointed out, that most other states adhered to the restatement rule, but in Pennsylvania the *Falchetti* decision expressly rejected this principle. Claytor found no justification for "Justice Black's theory" that there might have been something in the facts of the case that might give Tompkins recovery if given another trial. A Pennsylvania court, based upon the record "would have unquestionably" held that "Tompkins . . . was guilty of contributory negligence . . . [because] Pennsylvania has always had a very strict rule regarding [such cases]." Finally, the clerk concluded that, despite these considerations, "I suppose that a new trial must be granted."[60]

The material in Claytor's memo was not worked immediately into Brandeis' drafts. The justice incorporated information from Dobie's *Virginia Law Review* article of 1930, citing the "Seven Implications of *Swift* v. *Tyson.*" These criticisms included: "the notion as to the existence of a higher law that is non-territorial, to which . . . the federal court will resort," the extension of the doctrine in *Gelpcke,* the relative value of uniform federal common law as compared with a conflict of rules between state and federal law, and the "peculiar" ideas of Story. Dobie stressed that Story's interpretation of section 34 was unconstitutional (though congressional proposals aimed at destroying *Swift* by reducing diversity jurisdiction were "unwise"). Brandeis included

these views in his draft, citing as further authority the extension of *Swift* in the *Jensen, Gelpcke,* and *Burgess* v. *Seligman*
cases. At this point Brandeis cited one or two articles defending *Swift,* apparently in order to bring a degree of balance to his argument.[61]

In the fifth printed draft Brandeis integrated the summary of the facts with his statement of the broader jurisprudential and constitutional issues digested from Dobie, Johnson, the nineteenth-century writers and others. For the first
time in the drafting process a sentence beginning the opinion states the central issue in the case: "The question for
decision is whether the oft-challenged doctrine of *Swift* v.
Tyson shall now be disapproved." The justice included also
Story's construction of section 34, referring to the "frequent" expressions of doubt as to the "correctness" of the
view established in 1842. In another draft Brandeis introduced Charles Warren's discovery of the earlier version of
section 34 as further proof of Story's error. In this draft,
the justice developed more fully the dimension of his opinion concerning the problems following the extension of the
Swift doctrine. He noted the difficulties that arose in distin-
guishing the limits of local and general law, the violation of
the "fundamental requirement" of uniform doctrine within
the state, the denial of equal protection of law, the injustices
deriving from favoring the rights of non-residents over locals, and the subversion of the diversity of citizenship clause
of the Constitution.[62]

Along with this registry of errors, the justice cited
Holmes' dissent in the taxicab case, regarding the "unconstitutionality" of Story's "fallacy" of general law in construing section 34. There was "nothing in the constitution" justifying Story's distinction between general and local law,
said Brandeis. This was a question involving the "authority
by which particular acts . . . are governed," and, except
where federal questions were present, the only authority
was that of the state legislature and judiciary. "For there is
no other authority," Brandeis emphasized, "Congress, con-
fessedly, has no power to declare the law called general, be

it commerical or a part of the law of torts. And no clause of the constitution purports to confer such a power upon the federal courts." Given these considerations, the justice concluded with Holmes that the *Swift* doctrine represented "an unconstitutional assumption of powers by courts of the United States which no lapse of time or respectable array of opinion should make us hesitate to correct."[63]

Brandeis developed further the constitutional issues implicit in the *Swift* problem. The justice conceded, as Pepper and others had suggested, that jurisprudential conditions in the early republic may have justified Story's decision on the grounds of policy. But "experience in applying" the doctrine "revealed," he said, "its defects, political and social." A major "defect" involved the practice of corporations, seeking the more favorable general law, to reincorporate in states other than that of their original incorporation, solely for the purpose of establishing diversity jurisdiction (as had occurred in the taxicab case). Such practices had led to numerous attempts at "abolishing or limiting" diversity jurisdiction. Implying that he recognized that legislative efforts to end this subversion of federal jurisdiction had been unsuccessful, Brandeis affirmed that, "We need not determine whether the objections disclosed by experience are alone sufficient reason for abandoning a doctrine so widely applied throughout nearly a century." The "unconstitutionality of the course pursued," the justice exclaimed, "has now been made clear, and compels us to do so." This conclusion seems to draw partly upon Holmes' dissents and the analysis of Dobie and others that the abuse of diversity jurisdiction constituted an unconstitutional act.[64]

By March 17 Brandeis had written at least 13 drafts of his opinion, culminating in what he hoped would be the near-final version. Heading this draft, the justice inserted the date March 28, the Monday on which the decision would be read. Copies of the opinion were made and circulated among the other members of the Court. The replies indicated that the Justice's labors were not yet completed.[65]

On March 21, Reed wrote Brandeis giving his views con-

cerning the *Erie* opinion. Reed thought it "splendid." He
was "particularly glad" that no effort had been made to "determine the Pennsylvania law. My own doubts on that controlled my vote in conference." But the new justice had reservations about "an expression or two" that required
"modification . . . to make clear [that] there is no denial of
Congressional power to fix rules of law for Federal courts."
Brandeis' statement that Congress lacked the power to declare rules of common law, and that *Swift* had proclaimed
an unconstitutional course of action troubled Reed. "If it
meant," said Reed, "the *Swift* v. *Tyson* opinions are errors of
judges in construing Section 34, I quite agree but question
the advisability of calling such action 'unconstitutional.'"
The justice expressed the view that under the diversity
clause of Article III of the Constitution Congress possessed
the power to "prescribe the applicable law in the trials."
Reed wrote Brandeis: "It does not seem to me Justice
Holmes means more . . . than that the Courts act unconstitutionally when they wrongly determine statutes and
thereby assume powers." The justice concluded that he was
aware that overruling "a longstanding statutory interpretation is ordinarily questionable," but this seemed "a justifia-
ble exception." Soon thereafter, Reed wrote Brandeis that
he intended to circulate a "short concurrence."[66]

Brandeis replied to Reed's letter, defending his formulation of the constitutional issues raised by *Swift* and their relation to congressional authority. His opinion did not, said
the Justice, "pass upon or discuss the constitutionality of
section 34 as construed in *Swift* v. *Tyson*." It was "addressed
to showing that the action of the Court in disregarding state
law is unconstitutional. Since it admits," concluded Brandeis, "that the state rule must be followed if declared in a
statute, it admits that it is not a matter within the authority
of Congress."[67]

Reed's concurrence showed that he was unpersuaded by
Brandeis' answer. He accepted the overruling of the *Swift*
precedent based upon a reinterpretation of the word *laws*
in section 34; he denied the existence of a general juris-

prudence that was outside the language of the statute. Reed believed that it was unnecessary to go further than this, as Brandeis had done, proclaiming that Story's construction had been unconstitutional. "The effect of the opinion is not," said the Justice, "to interpret section 34 . . . but to declare it invalid, in toto, an unintentonal injury."[68]

On March 22, Black had written Brandeis. He considered the justice's *"requiem* over *Swift* v. *Tyson"* one of his "best— and that is saying much." Black, unlike Reed, had less serious (though to his mind no doubt just as significant) reservations about parts of the opinion. "I hope," he said, "that there may be no misunderstanding as to the application *to this particular case* which might bring about an unintentioned injury to the injured litigant." Black asked Brandeis to insert in his opinion something to show that the Court realized that the applicability of the *Falchetti* rule was open to question, suggesting a basis for retrial. Brandeis was amenable to this and had his clerk draft several lines (inserted in the final opinion) that the Court did not consider whether the Pennsylvania law prevented Tompkins' recovery.[69]

But it was Justice Stone's reply in two letters that led to the most substantive changes in the draft of the opinion marked for delivery on March 28. On March 23 Stone wrote Brandeis that although he did not have the opinion before him, he was concerned that the opinion stated "in effect" that there was "no constitutional power in Congress to require federal courts to apply rules of law inconcistent [sic] with those in force in the State, unless Congress is acting under one of the substantive powers granted to the national government." The justice admitted that this "may be so," but he felt uneasy about stating it "partly because it is unnecessary to do so" and because, for Stone, the matter was not "entirely free from doubt—the power may be implicit in the judicial sections." Also, he was "apprehensive of a doctrine which would require this Court constantly, without any aid from Congress, to draw the line between the rules of law applied by the federal courts which are substan-

tive and those which are procedural." Stone asked Brandeis
to eliminate or rephrase the lines.[70]

On March 24 the two justices talked further about the
matter; the next day Stone wrote Brandeis another letter.
Since his original note and their conversation, Stone told
Brandeis he had read the opinion and compared it with
Reed's concurrence. The justice agreed with Brandeis that
given the "long history of our support of *Swift* v. *Tyson*," he
saw "the force of the constitutional aspects of the case as an
impelling reason for overruling" the old precedent. He
thought it also vital, however, that the opinion "should not
discuss the constitutional question unless we definitely con-
clude that without it we would not overrule the precedents
of one hundred years."[71]

With this, Stone urged a change in Brandeis' phraseology. The *original* lines read: "We need not determine
whether the objections disclosed by experience are alone
sufficient reason for abandoning a doctrine so widely applied throughout nearly a century. For the unconstitutionality of the course pursued has now been made clear and
compels us to do so." These sentences followed the justice's
discussion of efforts to overrule *Swift* through congressional
action. Stone's rephrasing changed this focus, incorporating
an answer to Reed's argument that the overruling of *Swift*
was merely a matter of interpreting section 34. "If only a
question of statutory construction were involved we would
not be prepared to abandon a doctrine so widely applied
throughout nearly a century. But the unconstitutionality of
the course pursued has now been made clear and compels
us to do so." Both versions accept the view that *Swift* involved an unconstitutional exercise of power by the federal
courts. When the first is considered in the context of the
opinion draft, it seems apparent, however, that Brandeis
originally was emphasizing the fact that Congress had been
unable to halt this unconstitutional process, leaving the matter to the Court. Stone's change, as noted, actually addresses Reed's views. This alteration in focus seemed ac-

ceptable to Brandeis, for he inserted Stone's language into his opinion.[72]

Justice Butler prepared a comprehensive dissent challenging every point of Brandeis' opinion. The case was a "simple one," Butler said, involving the negligence of Tompkins in causing the accident. Most of the dissent criticized the opinion's emphasis upon the constitutional standing of *Swift* and the relation of this to the authority of Congress. Since "no constitutional question was suggested or argued" in either the lower court or the briefs of final appeal to the Supreme Court, Brandeis had gone beyond customary principles of adjudication. The *Swift* precedent had been followed, said Butler, in an "unbroken line" of decisions. He dismissed Brandeis' reference to Field's dissent in 1892 as an anomaly, given the fact that Field had applied the doctrine frequently in numerous decisions. Although Holmes had often dissented in the Court's application of *Swift,* the justice pointed out, he had been willing to accept it in commercial cases. Concerning Warren's research on section 34, Butler proclaimed that it did not "purport to be authoritative and was intended to be no more than suggestive." He stressed that the relevance of the research never had been considered by the Court, thereby casting doubt on the legitimacy of using it as a prop for a constitutional decision.[73]

Butler's firmest objection, however, involved what Brandeis had said concerning the power of Congress to establish rules of decision for federal courts. The language implied, said the justice, that section 34, as construed for nearly a century was "unconstitutional" and that federal judges were "now bound to follow decisions of the courts of the state . . . and that Congress is powerless otherwise to ordain." It was, prophesied Butler (echoing Miller's dissent in *Gelpcke* in 1864), "hard to foresee the consequences of the radical change so made." Further, Butler exclaimed, the Court should have moved cautiously seeking the assistance of counsel in arguing the constitutional question. He even suggested that the majority opinion violated a 1937 federal statute requiring the Supreme Court to call in the attorney general before invalidating an act of Congress. "Plainly," said Butler, the opinion "strikes down as unconstitutional [section] 34 as construed by our decisions; it divests Congress of power to prescribe rules to be followed by federal courts when deciding questions of general law . . . [compelling federal judges] to follow decisions of the courts of a particular state." Finally, concluded Butler, Keindl's argument that *Swift* did not apply should have been accepted and the Court should have reversed the circuit court in favor of the railroad.[74]

"It does not seem to me," Brandeis wrote in an undated memorandum, "that Justice Butler's opinion requires any change in the statements in my opinion." He did, however, "think it would be helpful" to clarify several points. These clarifications suggest further the intent of the justice's decision. Brandeis incorporated a lengthy passage from Field's *Baugh* dissent concerning the unconstitutionality of the concept of general law into the final version of the opinion. Hughes had read this section at length in conference on April 9. The justice developed in greater depth the point that Story's views may have had some basis during an age in which "the common law of many if not most of the states was still embryonic." But, he exclaimed, conditions were certainly improved in the twentieth, justifying a reversal of Story's decision. He addressed in more detail the oft-stated argument in defense of *Swift,* that it had brought uniformity of doctrine in federal courts, by holding that "the immediate result of diversity and uncertainty within a single jurisdiction" was "too high a price."

To clarify his argument regarding the authority of Congress over rules of decision Brandeis made several significant changes. He removed from a note a comment on section 34 in *Mason* v. *United States* that stated: "The statute . . . is merely declarative of the rule which would exist in absence of statute." He added further a footnote stating that the lower court should have applied local law "considering itself for this purpose an inferior state tribunal." Near the end of the opinion he tried to clear up his view on section 34: "In disapproving that [the *Swift*] doctrine we do not hold unconstitutional section 34 . . . or any other Act of Congress. We merely declare that in applying the doctrine this Court and the lower courts have invaded rights which in our opinion are reserved by the Constitution to the several States."[75]

Each of these changes were put into the final opinion. But the memorandum included another passage, intended as note number 24, that was *not* added. It was important because it answered expressly Butler's and Reed's contention that the *Erie* decision involved the constitutionality of section 34. "This is not to say that [section] 34 is in any way unconstitutional. Under no interpretation can that statute be said to require the federal courts independently to decide questions of general law." Brandeis exclaimed that Story had not so construed the section. The Court had held "merely that it did not apply at all to the general unwritten or common law of the States, so that the rule of decision for the federal courts in such cases was untouched by legislation." This "erroneous" construction of the statute "as being inoperative," the justice continued, led the Court further to assume "the power to disregard applicable state decisions and so create what amounted to a national common law." It was, concluded Brandeis, "this assumption of power by the Court, not by Congress, which Mr. Justice Holmes declared to be unconstitutional."[76]

Except for this note, the final decision of *Erie Railroad* v. *Tompkins* included the majority views analyzed above. The official report of Reed's concurrence was somewhat more detailed than the draft circulated March 24. Butler's dissent joined in by Justice McReynold's included few modifications of his draft. Brandeis' opinion, which was delivered on Monday, April 25, included several substantive changes suggested by Stone and Black, and his own additions given in the updated memorandum. It presented, however, essentially the same constitutional and jurisprudential theory that had evolved in the drafts between February 28 and March 17, and had been finalized in the version marked for presentation nearly a month before, on March 28. Interestingly, both the March 28 and April 25 versions had written on the back expressions of agreement from Hughes, Stone, Black, and Roberts. Hughes wrote "Admirable—I agree" on the first and "An excellent burial service" on the second. Stone and Roberts wrote "I agree" on both. Black stated the same, noting that his dissent in the *Gamer* case earlier in the term, although not mentioning *Swift*, had been directed at the doctrine.[77]

Erie R.R. v. *Tompkins* was sent back to the circuit court, where Judge Swan held that, according to the new precedent, Pennsylvania law must govern the case. Tompkins became a trespasser, having no right of recovery against the railroad; he returned to Pennsylvania and to obscurity. Nemeroff, after initial reservation, continued legal practice and eventually established a prosperous New York City law firm. Aaron Danzig left the law for some years but returned and became Nemeroff's partner. Kiendl continued with his firm, though on some unknown day between 1938 and his death in 1976 he destroyed his file on the *Erie* case. The press ignored the decision until its importance was pointed out by Justice Stone, after which *The New York Times* published several stories. But perhaps the most prophetic remark concerning *Erie* was scribbled in the margin of Judge Mandelbaum's copy of 304 United States Reports sometime between 1938 and 1946:

"although before this [Erie] case I never heard of . . . ["the Swift Tyson case"] to be truthful and for the confusion this [Erie] decision brought about, it might have been better to leave it alone and stand by good old *Swifty*."[78]

THE MEANING OF ERIE R.R. V. TOMPKINS

The meaning of *Erie* was unclear in 1938. Charles Warren, James Willard Hurst, and others wrote Justice Brandeis privately, praising the decision. Robert H. Jackson, Solicitor General of the United States and then a justice of the Supreme Court, called the overruling of *Swift* "one of the most dramatic episodes in the history of the Supreme Court"; he questioned, however, the wisdom of resting the decision on constitutional grounds, suggesting that Justice Reed's approach would have avoided potential confusion. Augustus N. Hand wrote Frankfurter that "As for *Swift* v. *Tyson,* I really do not like the way it was handled by L.D.B. and much preferred Stanley Reed. To say that the court was acting unconstitutionally in making and adhering to a decision for one hundred years . . . was quite unnecessary." Professor Harry Shulman of Yale Law School disapproved of both Reed's and Brandeis' approach, arguing that the Court could have reversed *Swift* "on grounds of policy, leaving the statute as construed and the constitution undisturbed." Frankfurter felt that the result of *Erie* was positive, but wrote Stone that the reasoning in reaching the result—raising as it did questions concerning the constitutional authority of Congress to establish rules for federal courts in diversity cases—would create for the Court "a good deal of trouble." [79]

These comments reveal an inherent difficulty in evaluating the Court's *Erie* decision. Criticism of the *Swift* doctrine had mounted since the 1870s, reaching a crescendo following the taxicab case in 1928. The Court began retreating from its assertion of an independent judgment over general law by 1930; the decision in 1938 seemed the natural result of persistent efforts to achieve needed reform in the use of federal judicial power. Yet the particular argument of Brandeis' opinion (while generally applauded in its result) was greeted with surprise, caution, and uncertainty by the rank and file of the legal profession and such prominent scholars as Frankfurter and Shulman. This mixed response suggests that the Court's decision held implications that went beyond the simple reversal of a 96-year-old precedent.

There were three principal objections to Brandeis' opin-

ion. Butler stated the first in his dissent. The arguments of
the attorneys for the Erie Railroad and Tompkins had not
challenged the validity of the *Swift* doctrine; they had
merely disagreed as to its applicability in their particular litigation. The announcement that the question for decision is
whether the oft-challenged doctrine of *Swift* v. *Tyson* shall
now be disapproved violated, said Butler, a basic principle
of common-law adjudication, according to which courts determine only those issues raised by the parties to a suit.
Only in exceptional circumstances was it considered appropriate for judges to gratuitously introduce into their opinions questions that had not been argued by counsel. Due to
these considerations, said the justice, the Court should have
given the litigants an opportunity to address the constitutional grounds upon which Brandeis based his decision. Following the reversal in the circuit court, Tompkins' attorneys
appealed to the Supreme Court, aggressively arguing this
position; it was an argument, however, the Court refused to
hear.[80]

The second objection involved Brandeis' remarkable
pronouncement that the federal court's application of the
Swift doctrine for nearly a century had been in violation of
the Constitution. Never in the history of the Supreme Court
had a line of precedent been overruled on the grounds that
the "course pursued" was unconstitutional. Field's dissent
first introduced the idea in 1892, and Holmes repeated it in
famous dissents between 1904 and 1928; but the Supreme
Court never before (or since) *Erie* decided a case on the
basis of such a theory. The anomalous character of the argument, however, was less significant than the uncertain
principle it established. Did the majority opinion mean that,
in the absence of a federal question, federal courts had no
discretionary authority whatsoever to declare rules of decision, unless they were to be found in the local law of the
state? Ever since 1789 federal judges had applied their own
substantive rules in equity cases, irrespective of state law.
Did *Erie* mean that this action too was unconstitutional?
These were troubling, complicated, and important ques-

tions. Justice Reed seemed justified in expressing doubt as to "whether, in the absence of federal statutory authority, federal courts would be compelled to follow state decisions." There was, he pointed out in his concurrence, "sufficient doubt about the matter in 1789 to induce the first Congress to legislate [in section 34 of the Judiciary Act of 1789]."[81]

This objection was inextricably linked with a third: Brandeis' implication that Congress lacked authority to establish (in diversity cases) substantive rules of law. As we have seen, a fundamental assumption of American constitutionalism was that Congress did not possess the power to declare principles of state local law. There was no agreement (indeed, no attempt to determine) the extent to which this limitation controlled congressional authority to establish substantive rules for federal courts. On this point, Stone wrote Frankfurter shortly after the *Erie* decision, "I should have liked to have said . . . that it was unnecessary to say how far or to what extent Congress might legislate." He enlarged upon this comment several years later, emphasizing the extent to which the whole matter was shrouded in uncertainty. "I do not think it is at all clear that Congress could not apply (enact) substantive rules to be applied by Federal courts." "I think," he concluded, "that *Erie Railroad Co.* v. *Tompkins* did not settle that question, not withstanding some unfortunate dicta in the opinion." Stone had expressed precisely the same view in his memoranda to Brandeis during the drafting of the *Erie* opinion. Frankfurter perceived this problem, writing Stone that the decision put the Court in the business of "drawing lines between . . . procedure and substance, and all its foggy differences." Reed's concurrence simply repeated the common assumption: While the "line between procedural and substantive law is hazy, no one doubts federal power over procedure."[82]

These complex technical questions involved larger social and political issues. *Erie's* impact in redefining the character of American judicial federalism held vital implications for the functioning of the extensive regulatory and administrative structure created under the New Deal. The New Deal programs established federal control in economic and social matters that overlapped, duplicated, or superseded altogether state and local authority. An important dimension of these programs was congressional delegation of authority to the federal courts to adjudicate cases arising out of their operation. The laws creating this jurisdiction established substantive rules of process or relied upon the new Federal Rules of Civil Procedure; these laws also gave rise to increased business in national tribunals. As the federal government enlarged its sphere of authority in the states, questions involving the limits of congressional and federal judicial power over substantive rules of law seemed inevitable, given the *Erie* decision.[83]

The uncertainties of the *Erie* opinion also created problems for the conduct of national (especially corporate) business. As Moore, Judge Parker, and Brown pointed out, diversity jurisdiction and the *Swift* doctrine—which had made possible forum shopping—had contributed organizational flexibility and investment security to the development and operation of the nation's economic order. The contention of Norris, Frankfurter, and others that local uncertainty and prejudice had abated was no doubt partly accurate; the fact that nonresident corporations and their attorneys, however, found subtler forms of local antagonism suggests that the critics' views required qualification. *Erie* seemed to destroy forum shopping and the predictability that had been built up around the uniformity of general law in federal court. For attorneys faced with the prospects of defending nonresident corporations in local courts—after years of enjoying advantages made possible by the *Swift* doctrine—Brandeis' opinion was bad news indeed.[84]

These social and political considerations suggest the range and significance of issues underlying the intricacies of the *Erie* decision. Given the extent of criticism by the 1930s of the *Swift* doctrine, it was not surprising that the Court rejected Butler's defense of the general law. But the very fact that *Swift* had outlived its usefulness raises a perplexing question: Why did the Court base its opinion upon a controversial constitutional theory rather than the less-sensitive grounds set forth in Reed's concurring opinion? This was of course the very issue that tempered Frankfurter's, Shulman's, Jackson's, and others' enthusiasm for *Erie.* Even defenders of *Swift* were willing to reduce the abuses of forum shopping; Reed's approach would have permitted this without bringing in explosive questions involving congressional power and the unconstitutionality of nearly a century of precedents.

Having a choice, why did Brandeis choose the course he did in deciding *Erie R. R. v. Tompkins?* The drafts of Brandeis' opinion and the memoranda written in response to it suggest some answers to this question. The lengthy footnotes in the final decision fail to include references to Hare's *Constitutional Law,* Thayer's *Harvard Law Review* article on *Gelpcke* v. *Dubuque,* and Gray's *Nature and Sources of Law.* Yet, the justice's handwritten notes for the early drafts reveal that these were the sources used in developing the underlying theory of his opinion. As we have seen, each of these writers condemned *Swift* because it fostered forum shopping and produced conflicting decisions in local jurisdictions; their criticism, while varying in analysis, argued that, because of these results, Story's decision was contrary to the Constitution. Hare's analysis implied that *Swift* constituted an improper and arbitrary violation of state sovereignty. Thayer agreed, except that he accepted the need for a limited exercise of independent judgment where local law was "irrational." Gray deemphasized the constitutional argument, while stressing the anomalous character of Story's *Swift* doctrine. Despite differences in focus, each critic objected to abuses of federal jurisdiction made possible by *Swift,* and concluded that because of these results the doctrine violated fundamental principles of the nation's constitutional order. A preoccupation with the extension of *Swift* in the bond cases as evidence of unconstitutional use of federal judicial authority was another factor common to the analysis of these critics.

Other sources Brandeis used in this initial draft were Pepper's *Borderland of Federal and State Law,* Johnson's *Kentucky Law Review* article of 1929, Dobie's "Seven Implications of *Swift* v. *Tyson*" of 1930, and Shelton's 1928 *Virginia Law Review* essay. Pepper's treatise was of course influenced by Hare's analysis, stressing the constitutional dimensions of the *Swift* problem.[85] The approach of each of the articles relied heavily upon similar reasoning. Use of these sources strongly suggests Brandeis' perception of the fundamental problems raised by the *Swift* doctrine; it was a perception that the justice had written into a note appearing in a 1930 decision upholding local law (irregardless of *Swift* and *Gelpcke*). It was quite possible too that the justice's views had even deeper roots in his encounters with the general law as a law student in 1876. And, of course, Brandeis had concurred in several Holmes dissents holding that *Swift* was the basis of an unconstitutional course of decisions.

Thus, the justice's choice of sources suggests a partial explanation for his constitutional approach in *Erie.* Reliance upon the critical tradition represented by these sources may help explain further the meaning of Brandeis' reference concerning congressional authority to establish rules for federal courts. Commentators throughout the nineteenth century, like their counterparts writing after 1900 (including Justice Holmes), agreed that Congress could not declare substantive rules of local law. At the same time, however, as we have seen, no effort was made to distinguish between rules of substantive law and procedure (this was so largely because such a distinction was extremely difficult, if not impossible to determine). Brandeis refers to this issue twice in his opinion; in both instances the reference appears as a stated assumption, with no effort made to develop its implications. This parallels exactly the treatment of the question in Sergeant's treatise of 1830, Pepper's work of 1895, and the article of Johnson and Dobie after 1928. The implication here is that Brandeis in his *Erie* opinion did not attempt to settle or even address the tangled problem of congressional authority over substantive rules of law and procedure. He was simply stating as a premise a familiar assumption inherent in American constitutional law.[86]

Brandeis probably felt compelled to state this premise to strengthen his central proposition that the *Swift* doctrine was in violation of the constitution. In his reply to Reed's memoranda concerning the concurring opinion, Brandeis said so expressly: The opinion did not "pass on or discuss the constitutionality of section 34 as construed in *Swift* v. *Tyson.*" The decision was, emphasized the justice, "addressed to showing that the action of the Court in disregarding state law is unconstitutional. *Since it admits that the state rule must be followed if declared in a statute, it admits that it is not a matter within the authority of Congress.*" Here again Brandeis reveals the influence of the critics from whom he had drawn the theory underlying the *Erie* decision. A major preoccupation of these critics had been the extension of *Swift* in the bond cases. In *Gelpcke* and numerous other decisions, the Court had voided local courts' interpretations of state statutes and constitutions as unconstitutional. In effect these decisions were declaring substantive rules of local law. Reference to congressional power was made in this connection to highlight further the subtle fallacy of *Swift,* since it was relatively undisputed that Congress lacked authority to establish substantive principles of state law.[87]

In the memoranda written in response to Butler's dissent, Brandeis repeated this view. Section 34 was not "in any way unconstitutional." The Court had "erroneously . . . construed the statute as being inoperative . . . [and] went further and assumed the power to disregard applicable state decisions and so create what amounted to a national common law." It was, the justice stressed, *"this assumption of power by the Court, not by Congress which Mr. Justice Holmes declared to be unconstitutional."* The phrases borrowed verbatim from Stone may be considered in light of this analysis. As we have seen, Brandeis had said in the March 28 draft that it was unnecessary to "determine whether objections disclosed by experience are alone sufficient reason for abandoning a doctrine so widely applied throughout nearly a

century." He then asserted that the "unconstitutionality of
the course pursued has now been made clear and compels
us to do so." Stone urged a change which read, "If only a
question of statutory construction were involved, we should
not be prepared to abandon a doctrine so widely applied
throughout nearly a century." The purpose of the change
was to strengthen the wording by reference to the length of
time in which the error of *Swift* had been applied, thus justifying recourse to the Constitution. Brandeis probably accepted Stone's rephrasing because it did not alter his basic
intent, which was to eradicate an "unconstitutional course"
of judicial action. This was the central focus of the decision;
the Justice was probably essentially unconcerned with establishing the limits of congressional authority.[88]

Along with the reliance upon the late-nineteenth-century
critics of *Swift,* there were other factors that contributed to
the formulation of the *Erie* opinion. A belief in the value of
local development and customs was a moral principle for
Brandeis. Local statutes and common law embodied, the
justice believed, distinct "traditions" and "peculiar habits of
mind," manifesting a community's unique "spirit." These
values were inseparable from Brandeis' fundamental distrust of bigness and centralization, whether in business or
government. Only through "development of life" in the
states and localities was the achievement of "American ideals" possible, as a bulwark against the "curse of bigness."
Those close to Justice Brandeis knew that these were powerful and dynamic forces in his character; even a superficial
reading suggests that these convictions permeate *Erie R.R.
v. Tompkins.* Significantly, such values (differing perhaps in
levels of intensity) were to be found in the thinking of other
early twentieth century contemporaries. Beale apparently
shared similar views, Fordham's article in the *North Carolina
Law Review* reflected such notions, and a small but persistent group of "decentralist intellectuals" resisted the New
Deal. This simply suggests that the philosophical assumptions suffusing *Erie* were not unique to Brandeis.[89]

Another influence, vague but nonetheless implicit in the

opinion, was a concern for "defects, political and social," resulting from *Swift*. Unquestionably Brandeis and the majority in *Erie* shared with many members of the legal profession a distaste for the abuses of forum shopping illustrated
by the infamous taxicab decision of 1928. The sources cited
in the *Erie* opinion referring to these abuses and the 1928
precedent, however, evidence more than a concern for equity. We have noted that the public's persistent distrust of
law and lawyers was a familiar theme throughout the nation's history, into the twentieth century. Around the turn
of the century, the public's negative perception of the legal
profession was influenced in part by the close association of
lawyers with corporate business. Through sharp practices
(such as those used in the taxicab affair) lawyers enabled
corporations to manipulate the legal process, thus fostering
a general public disrespect for law. Judge Dawson, like
other authors cited by Brandeis, pointed out the connection
between *Swift* and the threat of social disorder.

There seems little doubt that this was an important issue
to Brandeis. The leading lawyers in the United States have
been, he wrote in 1905, "engaged mainly in supporting the
claims of corporations; often in endeavoring to evade or
nullify the . . . crude laws by which legislators sought to
regulate the power or curb the excesses of corporations."
The Kentucky statute that had led to the strategy used in
the taxicab suit qualified as such a law. The result had upset
Brandeis enough that he cooperated in efforts to draft
congressional legislation designed to prevent abuses of federal jurisdiction that had led to contravention of an explicit
state policy. But it was possible that there were still other
considerations at work here, for Brandeis (like Hare whom
he used in the opinion) perceived that a bar free from the
stigma of business manipulation was essential to the preservation of social peace in America. In 1893 Brandeis wrote
Charles W. Eliot, that the "conservativism that the study of
law fosters would, in the present ferment, be of great value
to the society." He was more explicit some years later. A
"revolt of the people against the capitalists, was inevitable,"

said the justice, "unless the aspirations of the people are
given some adequate legal expression; and to this end co-
operation of the abler lawyers is essential." Amidst the dislocation of the Great Depression, it seems not unlikely that
fears of social tension noted by Dawson and others were
among those political and social "defects" Brandeis hoped
to ameliorate in the *Erie* decision.[90]

Finally, the most explicit influence evident in the historic
decision of 1938 was the positivism of Oliver Wendell
Holmes. Brandeis cites Holmes' dissents in *Kuhn, Jensen,*
and the taxicab case several times throughout his opinion as
the source of the idea that the *Swift* doctrine represented an
unconstitutional exercise of federal judicial power. In 1928
Brandeis wrote Frankfurter that the justice's dissent "will
stand among his notable opinions," and that it was "delivered with fervor." The principal elements of Holmes' theory, as developed in letters to Pollock and Laski, included
the assumption that all law must have some sovereign authority behind it, that there was no general law separate
from or independent of this authority, that judges who asserted the existence of such a law violated tenets of legislative supremacy, and that the Constitution as originally conceived by the framers embodied these principles (at least to
the extent that they were at odds with Story's *Swift* opinion).[91]

Brandeis certainly accepted the essentials of this theory.
However, Holmes' influence was not the only (perhaps not
even the major) factor behind the particular jurisprudential
approach taken in the *Erie* decision. This is noteworthy because twentieth-century defenders of *Swift* v. *Tyson* used
reasoning derived from legal positivism, as did the critics of
the doctrine. Green and others argued that the *Swift* principle was consistent with a nationalist theory of sovereignty
and Yntema developed a persuasive historical analysis supporting this view. Corbin articulated what was probably the
profoundest refutation of the Holmesian analysis of *Swift,*
while drawing upon the basic positivistic assumptions that
the great legal thinker had done so much to establish.

These considerations point up the extent to which the *Erie* opinion and the theory underlying it were anchored in a current of legal theory that transcended the contribution of any single individual.[92]

Unquestionably, concern for inequities growing out of the *Swift* doctrine was a vital factor in bringing about the *Erie* decision. Important, too, was the Court's general retreat from direct involvement in the economy represented by its sanction of New Deal legislation after 1936. But the fact that the majority of the justices were unable to agree among themselves as to the particular form and content of the new approach to federal judicial authority suggests that other influences were instrumental in shaping the final opinion. Brandeis synthesized the similar but distinct approaches of Hare, Thayer, Pepper, Gray, Holmes and others in developing the basis for his reversal of *Swift* v. *Tyson*. These jurists had used positivistic assumptions to develop a unique analysis of the proper role of the federal courts in the federal system.

There was nothing compelling Brandeis to choose this particular analytical approach in formulating his decision. Reed's concurring opinion offered a reasonable and less rigid basis for overruling the old precedent. As the communication exchanged between Reed and Brandeis shows, Brandeis rejected Reed's views apparently because he believed that his sources embodied a "truer" conception of American federalism. This belief was perhaps reenforced by a deep personal commitment to values of localism, decentralism, and a concern for the role of the legal profession in maintaining social order. Faithful to these values, Brandeis subordinated Reed's concern for the working realities of implementing the *Erie* doctrine, to a deeper urge to establish a constitutional underpinning for a new judicial federalism. This suggests that *Erie* resulted primarily from a triumph of theory over function in the conceptualization of the proper limits of the federal system. It remained to be seen whether this conception of federalism would function any better than the one it overturned.

Chapter IV

Conclusions and Closed Options

There will remain the inevitable problem in a federal system that recurringly competing state interests . . . may have to be evaluated in the light of the national interest in interstate harmony. It is the classic political problem of weighing, adjusting, and harmonizing diverse community values.

Chief Justice Traynor
"Is This Conflict Really Necessary," 1959

Forty years after the decision of *Erie* v. *Tompkins* the legal landscape including federal jurisdiction over the common law had changed considerably. Federal intervention in the economic and social affairs of Americans had grown to a point probably inconceivable to either defenders or opponents of the New Deal. Diversity jurisdiction and state law, once the major source of litigation in federal court, although still important, was superseded by spiraling categories of "federal questions" arising out of national regulations, statutes, civil rights, and the "new" federal common law. But even though federalization of the nation's law narrowed the reach of the *Erie* doctrine, the need to balance and adjust state and national interests as manifested in traditional common-law litigation persisted.[1] A history of the *Swift* and *Erie* cases lends perspective to this dimension of American federalism, but it also suggests broader implications involving the operation of legal institutions in a changing society. Tracing the origin, decision, and evolution of the Story and Brandeis opinions provides one illuminating example of the extent to which law interacted with, influenced, and was influenced by social, political, and economic realities from the early days of the republic to the last third of the twentieth century.

During the early nineteenth century the displacement of general merchants by specialized middlemen was part of a major transformation in the nation's economic order. The federal courts contributed to this transformation by reducing the uncertainties of interstate credit transactions through resolution of mercantile litigation on the basis of general principles of commercial law. The decision of *Swift* v. *Tyson* in 1842 was the culmination of 50 years of federal judicial response to the changing needs of national business. Given the uncertainty of state law and the persistence of erratic local prejudice there seems little doubt that federal court's administration of negotiability and other commercial principles reduced the costs of interstate trade and aided economic development. This contribution to commercial stability also probably helped to maintain the social and political preeminence of merchants.

The enlargement of the general law, particularly between 1860 and the 1890s seemed to have had a similar impact on the rise of large-scale corporate enterprise. State and local governments' attempted enforcement of bond repudiations, and local jury's and certain elected judiciary's almost certain distrust of "foreign" corporations in fellow servant cases, suggested that localism threatened to impede national business development in the postbellum period. The federal judiciary's adjudication of bond and fellow-servant cases, as well as some 26 other categories of diversity litigation, no doubt reduced the uncertainties interstate corporate enterprises faced during these years. This conclusion is reinforced by the fact that business leaders expressly stated their preference for federal courts in trials of these and other questions. In the twentieth century, with the improved sophistication of the administration of state law and the reduction (if not extinction) of local prejudice—along with the unparalleled growth of federal regulation—the connection between federal jurisdiction and interstate business became less explicit.

The issue of common-law jurisdiction also carried intriguing implications for the public image of the bar and legal education and their relationship to social order. The conception of general law as evidence of universal standards of mercantile behavior corresponded with the perception of lawyers as disinterested technicians, a view that became popular during the Age of Jackson. According to this view, lawyers discovered neutral principles and applied them to commercial cases, taking little or no notice of their general social or political consequences. From the 1870s to the 1930s a division of opinion developed among lawyers based in part upon disagreement over the *Swift* doctrine. Defenders emphasized the flexibility and predictability the doctrine gave litigants in federal court; critics, however, condemned the sharp practices built up around *Swift*. The critics claimed that such practices weakened the citizen's respect for law (and the legal profession), thus opening the way for the forces of disorder.

Questions involving the status of state law in federal court have had significant impact on the relationship between legal education and judicial policy. It should not seem surprising that Story's opinion followed years of commentary by DuPenceau, Tucker, Rawles, Sergeant, Sullivan and others arguing for the construction of section 34 established in 1842. Story cited DuPonceau and Rawles in his decision. The influence of the *Swift* principle spread through the writing and teaching of Kent and Story, who referred to it in their classrooms and cited it in treatises that were used in law offices throughout the country. Following the Civil War, Thayer and Hare influenced a whole generation of lawyers, including George Wharton Pepper, Brandeis, Richard Henry Beale, Felix Frankfurter and many others. After the turn of the century the critical tradition was carried on by Gray, Beale, Frankfurter, Warren and others. As we have seen, Brandeis drew upon Hare, Thayer, and Gray for the underlying theory of his *Erie* opinion. From 1938 on, this conception has influenced new generations of law students encountering it for the first time in federal jurisdiction, conflict of law, and, of course, civil procedure classes.

The evolution of the *Swift* and *Erie* doctrines have been

important too because they reflect more general changes in jurisprudential thinking throughout the nation's history. Shortly after the Court announced its opinion in 1938, Frankfurter summarized his view of the broad change in a letter to Stone. As you well know, he wrote, "there has been an enormous shift in juristic outlook between Story's day and ours, and I have very little doubt that scholarly exploration . . . of the juristic atmosphere which Story and his colleagues breathed would support Story's notion that 'laws' meant something like natural law. . . . In other words, such decisions were merely evidence of 'law' and not the 'law.' "[2] It seems apparent that, despite Frankfurter's assertion, natural law assumptions did not underlie Story's opinion. But Frankfurter's emphasis upon a shift in jurisprudential thought deserves attention nevertheless. There were in fact several stages of legal thinking that influenced the transformation of the *Swift* doctrine and the decision of *Erie* v. *Tompkins*.

Antebellum commercial journals and commentators assumed that court decisions were evidence of principles of general commercial practice, though they never resolved whether judicial precedent or mercantile custom were the surest guide to what these principles were. Following the Civil War, amidst increasing emphasis on sovereignty and territoriality in legal thought, the underlying assumptions concerning the existence of general standards of mercantile practice were undermined. Replacing them were ambiguous notions upon which both critics and defenders of the general law based their arguments. Thayer and Grosscup, Miller, and eventually Field believed that only the law of the state could provide rules in diversity cases. They admitted, however, that state decisions were actually mirrors of what the local law was in fact, and that federal judges possessed the authority to declare this law where it was unclear or unreasonable. Hare, Meigs, Holmes, and others were proponents of a legal positivism which not only denied the existence of a general jurisprudence, but refused to sanction any independent judgment as to what constituted the local law. Defenders of *Swift* such as Shiras, Brewer, and Taft applied notions of national sovereignty to justify the doctrine as a formalistic device for evolving a uniform common law in federal courts.

Following the turn of the century Thayer's views persisted in the thinking of Beale, as did Brewer's notion of a constitutional basis for a national common law. It was, however, the positivism of Holmes and Gray that came to dominate legal thought in the twentieth century. Both defenders and critics of *Swift* resorted to positivism in their debate over the theory underlying the doctrine. Brandeis, of course, while citing Holmes' dissents at length, synthesized the ideas of Hare, Thayer, and Gray in formulating the basic argument of the *Erie* opinion. Thus, even though positivistic assumptions suffused the decision, it reflected more complex origins and diverse strains of jurisprudential thinking. A philosophical preoccupation with the virtues of local customs and values favoring decentralization undoubtedly contributed to the result as well.

By the last third of the century, scholarly analysis of *Erie* suggested that yet another change in legal theory was underway. Beginning in the 1850s the question of common-law jurisdiction became inextricably connected with its constitutional justification. Because the thinking of Story and his predecessors was absorbed in particular assumptions concerning the nature of law, their theorizing about federal jurisdiction over the common law did not reach the constitutional question. Jeffersonians such as Tucker, Johnson, and Daniel readily accepted the idea of general commercial law, without perceiving any issues of states' rights. But as the Taney Court faced the implications of slavery in the mid-1850s, and following the impact of the Civil War and rise of a national economic order, the focus of theorizing about *Swift* became the Constitution. This concern was a major dimension of the Erie decision.

After 1938 the Court was unwilling to confront the constitutional implications of *Erie,* satisfied instead with policing forum shopping and other inequities. But by the 1950s the constitutional implications were again pressing to the fore. By the 1970s much of the analysis of the role of *Erie* in the federal system dealt with constitutional themes (though in quite intricate terms). As centralization of the federal government continued unabated, this renewed attention to the balance of federal and state authority under the Constitution seemed most appropriate. Professor H. M. Hart captured the central theme of this process. "Ours, therefore, is the continuing task," he said, "of trying to mature and perfect this compound system, so as to liquidate the meaning of all its parts and adjust them to each other in a harmonious and consistent whole. We may debate, as we must, what conception of the role of the federal courts under this Constitution best fits these requirements." But, he concluded, "we know in advance that any role which is inharmonious and inconsistent cannot have been the intended one."[3]

This tension between harmony and dissonance touches the very essence of American federalism; it concerns a determination of the limits of power of state and national government. The *Swift* and *Erie* decisions embodied different approaches to this difficult but important problem. In *Swift* the Court formulated a theory that extended federal jurisdiction as far as but not beyond the limits of national power established under the commerce clause. This emphasized the outer limits of federal judicial power. *Erie* set forth a principle aimed at binding federal courts to state law; its intent was the obliteration of judicial discretion in diversity cases. But despite divergent results, the Court's purpose in both decisions was to establish constitutional limits governing the role of the national judiciary within the federal system.

The perception of the need to address the constitutional issues arising out of federal jurisdiction over state law changed between 1842 and 1938. Contemporary conceptions of commercial jurisprudence and the source and nature of law meant that Story and his states' rights colleagues viewed federal-state relations as a secondary and largely implicit question in the *Swift* case. The Civil War, the emergence of a national corporate economy, and the influence of new schools of legal thought undermined the metaphysical foundations of *Swift*. As this process continued between the 1860s and the Great Depression, the constitutional issues that had been implicit in 1842 became increasingly the center of attention. Given the constitutionalisation of the *Swift* doctrine and the fundamental changes occurring with the revolution of 1936 and 1937, the Supreme Court's emphasis upon the constitutional themes inherent in the *Erie* case was not surprising.

As critics were quick to point out, however, the tone of the *Erie* opinion was too unequivocal. This was no doubt due to Brandeis' deep-felt need to support values favoring local control and decentralized governmental authority. But its overly rigid form should not obscure the central purpose of the decision: the affirmation of the principle of constitutional limitation in the nation's federal system. Following the opinions of Taft, Shiras, Brewer, and others the federal courts had lost touch completely with the original intent of *Swift*. With the taxicab decision of 1928, the potential reach of federal judicial power seemed unrestricted. During the early 1930s the Court backed off somewhat from applying *Swift*, but was unwilling to deal directly with the threat the doctrine posed for the principle of limited federal power. When the Court finally upheld an unprecedented extension of national power in 1936, the status of the principle of constitutional limitation had become quite precarious.

With these developments in the forefront, the constitutional thrust of the *Erie* decision was both understandable and justified. Justice Reed of course argued the wisdom of ignoring the constitutional question; he advised putting *Swift* to rest through a process of statutory construction. Frankfurter and others concurred. But the impact of Reed's approach on the already uncertain condition of constitutional limitation should be pondered. In *Erie* the Court was given the opportunity not only to erradicate the abuses growing out of *Swift*, but also to assert a more general theory of the character of American federalism. Reed's approach would have satisfied the first goal but done nothing to further the second.

The argument that *Erie* was intended as a constitutional decision is supported by consideration of Justice Stone's influence on the final form of the opinion. Stone did not share Brandeis' decentralist, localist values; but he did believe that an extension of national power should take place within the broad framework of constitutional limitations. After the Court's sanction of the New Deal in 1936 and 1937, it was unclear whether the commerce clause, the Fourteenth Amendment, or even some *Swift*-like common law would serve as the main constitutional basis for enlarged federal authority.

Given the abuses of *Swift* the common-law approach as administered by federal courts was untenable. But the right of Congress to give federal judges the authority to develop a body of common-law rules was more unclear. It was of course concerning this uncertain point that Stone, during the drafting of the *Erie* opinion, urged Brandeis to adopt clarifying language. Brandeis probably believed that Congress lacked the power to give federal courts a broad common-law power (he had, after all, opposed the federal code of civil procedure on the grounds that it was unconstitutional). Faced, however, with Reed's disagreement and the dissent of Butler and McReynolds the justice could not afford to fragment the *Erie* majority further by ignoring Stone's suggestions. Stone's changes created the basis for controversy in later years. If, however, Brandeis had had his way the issue may well have become even more controversial because under the justice's original draft it appeared that congressional authority was so limited as to be virtually nonexistent.

Stone's insistence that Brandeis state flatly that congressional authority was not at issue in *Erie* may have represented, then, an attempt to clarify a difficult and pressing problem. Stone may have been trying also to remove doubts concerning federal power under the commerce clause and the Fourteenth Amendment. Following the dramatic shift in Supreme Court policy during 1936 and 1937, a pervasive uncertainty existed as to the limits of national power. Although the commerce clause would evolve as the primary constitutional sanction for enlarged federal authority, this was neither obvious nor certain during the mid and late 1930s. Thus, as he had with regard to the issue of common-law jurisdiction, Justice Stone may have been trying in his revisions of *Erie* to keep congressional options open.[4]

At the same time, however, Stone (as suggested in his letters to Frankfurter) seemed unwilling to go entirely toward Reed's direction by holding that there was no issue of constitutional limitation present at all in the *Erie* case. Stone's comments on *United States* v. *Caroline Products Co.* (decided during the same term as *Erie*) revealed his fear that the necessities of enlarged congressional power could be used to justify a subversion of free government. "I have been deeply concerned," he wrote Judge Irving Lehman concerning the decision, "about the increasing racial and religious intolerance which seems to bedevil the world, and which I greatly fear may be augmented in this country. For that reason I was greatly disturbed by the attacks on the Court and the Constitution last year, for one consequence of the program of 'judicial reform' might well result in breaking down the guaranties of individual liberty." The justice's lone dissent in the first flag salute case a year and a half later revealed the extent to which these values were in the forefront of his thinking during this period.[5]

The *Swift* decision as originally conceived in 1842 was intended to sanction federal adjudication of interstate commercial transactions, while upholding state power. A reading of Stone's role in *Erie* suggests that in 1938 the Court was again attempting to accommodate the limits of state and federal authority to the changing needs of the nation's constitutional order. The Court was presented with a choice between ignoring or facing squarely the difficult but important constitutional issues raised in the *Erie* case. By choosing the constitutional ground for its decision, the Court created the terms of an inevitable debate over the proper limits of national and state power within the federal system. Institutionalizing this debate no doubt fostered inefficiencies, but it also insured that governmental action would be held accountable to the principle of constitutional limitations. The value of this result points towards the importance of the *Swift* and *Erie* cases in American federalism.

Notes

LIST OF ABBREVIATIONS FOR JOURNAL TITLES

ABAJ	American Bar Association Journal
ALR	American Law Review
CLJ	Central Law Journal
HLR	Harvard Law Review
Hunt's	Hunt's Merchants' Magazine
I.L.J.	Indiana Law Journal
Ky.L.J.	Kentucky Law Journal
NAR	North American Review
NYULR	New York University Law Review
Un.Pa.L.Rev.	University of Pennsylvania Law Review
Vir.L.Rev.	Virginia Law Review

CHAPTER I

1. *Erie R. Co.* v. *Tompkins* 304 U.S. 65 (1938). See chapters 2 and 3 for the origin of the dominant interpretation of *Swift*.

2. Morton J. Horwitz, *The Transformation of American Law, 1780–1860* (Cambridge, Mass., 1977), 245–52.

3. *United States* v. *Worral*, 2 Dallas 384 (1798); *United States* v. *Hudson*, 7 Cranch 32 (1812); *United States* v. *Coolidge*, 1 Wheaton 415 (1816); Julius Goebel, Jr., *Antecedents and Beginnings: The Oliver Wendell Holmes Devise History of the Supreme Court of the United States*, (Paul A. Freund ed., New York, 1971), I, 608–62. See Chapters 2 and 3 for a discussion of numerous commentators on and critics of *Swift*, especially Charles Warren, Felix Frankfurter, William W. Crosskey, and others. Randall Bridwell and Ralph U. Whitten, *Constitution and the Common Law: The Decline of Doctrines of Separation of Powers and Federalism* (Lexington, 1977) in some ways parallels and in other ways differs from the analysis given here. My *Forums of Order: The Federal Courts and Business in American History* (Greenwich, 1979), 53 gives essentially a functional analysis of *Swift*. While the present study modifies and broadens the interpretation given in the earlier work, and whereas the two tend to emphasize different perspectives, they are basically consistent in their overall conclusion concerning the meaning of *Swift*. See also Grant Gilmore, *The Ages of American Law* (New Haven, 1978); Tony Freyer, "The Social Matrix of Legal Change," *Reviews in American History*, VII (September 1979), 319–24; Mark Tushnet, "*Swift* v. *Tyson* Exhumed," *Yale Law Journal*, 79 (1969), 284–93; Charles A. Heckman, "Uniform Commercial Law in the Nineteenth Century Federal Courts: The Decline and Abuses of the *Swift* Doctrine," *Emory Law Journal*, 27 (1978), 45–66.

4. See below for a thorough consideration of this question.

5. John Frank, *Justice Daniel Dissenting: A Biography of Peter v. Daniel, 1784–1860*

(Cambridge, 1964) shows how badly misled later critics of *Swift* were as a result of their preoccupation with the excesses of *Swift* in their own day. "*Swift* v. *Tyson* is a perfect illustration of the error which lies in reading the views of one generation back into the views of another. In 1938 this case was over-ruled, on the ground, among others, that it was severely incompatible with the right of the states to make their own law. In short it was found that a strongly states' rights Court had given too much power to the Federal Government. The opinion of Justice Brandeis to the effect that the Constitution requires application of state laws appears to be precisely what Daniel would have said—*if he had thought of it. As Daniel did not dissent there could not have been much of a states' rights issue in the case as originally conceived.*" Italics added, 168–69. Daniel was perhaps the most states' rights-minded judge ever to sit on the Supreme Court.

6. "The Law of Nations as a Part of the National Law of the United States," *University of Pennsylvania Law Review* 101 (1952–53), 26–96, 792–833.

7. Ibid., 794–95, 797–800.

8. Some of the generalizations in the following pages derive from more detailed evidence given in my *Forums of Order*. Where this is the case I will usually cite only the appropriate pages in that book (except where a direct quote from a primary source is given).

9. The following narrative of the facts of *Swift* case has been drawn from: "Manuscript Record of the Case of *Swift* v. *Tysen*" (CCDNY, 1837–40)." These manuscripts include numbered, dated, unnumbered, and undated files and affidavits; and are located in the National Archives in Washington. The records of "The Supreme Court of the United States," #68, *Joseph Swift* v. *George W. Tysen*, "in the United States Records and Briefs, part 1, Jan. 1841 to Jan. 1843," Vol. 1, 1–14, located at the University of Pennsylvania Law School, and Reel #7 of the microfilm series of the Scholarly Resources Inc. were also used. See also, *Swift* v. *Tyson* 16 Peters 1 (1842). Except where reference is made to the title of 16 Peters 1 itself, I have used the spelling of Tysen given in the manuscript records. The spelling of "Tyson" in 16 Peters 1 was quite likely a recorder's error, or by 1842 Tysen himself may have changed the spelling. In most instances, except where a direct quote is given or in other exceptional cases, I have left the sources of the facts of the case uncited. For a complete citation see Tony Freyer, "Unity From Diversity: Commercial Stability and *Swift* v. *Tyson* (1842) (Ph.D. diss., Indiana University, 1975), 1–28, which, revised, is Chapter V in *Forums of Order*.

10. *Forums of Order*, 1–18, for full discussion of legal character of credit relations and their significance in the antebellum business order.

11. Ibid., 36–52. The following discussion is drawn from these pages and those cited in note 10.

12. Francis Upton, "The Law of Debtor and Creditor in Louisiana," *Hunt's* XV (July 1846), 70.

13. "Law Reform," *Hunt's* VII (December 1842), 535.

14. *Hunt's* XX (April 1849), 388.

15. Hopkinson, "Commercial Integrity," *Hunt's* I (November 1839), 375.

16. Benjamin F. Porter, "Commerce and the Prejudice Against It," *Hunt's* XIX (October, 1848), 392–393.

17. See notes 10 and 11.

18. *Warren* v. *Lynch*, 5 Johns, 239 (1810), *Bay* v. *Coddington*, 5 Johns. Chancery Rep. 54 (1821), *Bay* v. *Coddington*, 20 Johns. Ct. of Errors Rep. 637 (1821), *Wardell* v.

Howell, 9 Wend. 170 (1827); *Rosa v. Brotherson*, 10 Wend. 85 (1833), *Ontario Bank v. Worthington*, 12 Wend. 593 (1834), *Payne v. Cutler*, 13 Wend. 605 (1834), *Smith v. Van Loan*, 16 Wend. 659 (1837), *Bank of Salina v. Babcock*, 21 Wend. 499 (1839), *Bank of Sandusky v. Scoville*, 24 Wend. 115 (1840).

19. Hessel E. Yntema and George H. Jaffin, "Preliminary Analysis of Concurrent Jurisdiction," *University of Pennsylvania Law Review* LXXIX (May 1931), 85–86.

20. See *Forums of Order*, 53–72 for full discussion of litigation in the lower court.

21. *U.S. Statutes at Large*, I, 92.

22. See *Forums of Order*, 73–76 for discussion of argument in the Supreme Court. Fessenden's quote, *Swift v. Tyson*, 16 Peters 8 (1842).

23. 16 Peters 5.

24. Ibid., 12.

25. The following discussion of Story's opinion follows in part that given in *Forums of Order*, 77–89. But, as noted above, I have in the present argument developed more fully the jurisprudential themes and have thus changed the emphasis of the analysis. Citation is at 16 Peters 18.

26. 16 Peters 18–19.

27. Ibid., 20.

28. Ibid., 23.

29. See Charles Warren, *The Supreme Court in American History*, 3 vols. (Boston, 1923), II, 363 for newspaper reference; for law journal cite see, "Bills of Exchange," *Pennsylvania Law Journal* I (1842), 219. The reference to Story's use of *Swift* in class is "Judge Story's Note of Argument in Moot Court, Spring Term, 1842." I am indebted to Miss Edith Henderson of the Treasure Room at Harvard Law School for this reference.

30. Hilliard, *Elements of Law*, 227; *Providence Journal*, as quoted in *Niles' Weekly Register*, December 3, 1925; "Debtor-Creditor Laws of Alabama," *Hunt's*, VI (February 1842), 156. Story, *Commentaries on the Constitution*, 3 vols. (Boston, 1833), III, 564.

31. Abel P. Upshur, *A Brief Enquiry into the True Nature and Character of Our Federal Government; Being a Review of Judge Story's Commentaries on the Constitution of the United States* (Petersburg, 1840), 83; Wallace, *Commercial Law*, 54.

32. "The American Jurist," *NAR* XXIX (Oct. 1829), 422.

33. Matthew Carey, "Reports of Cases Argued and Adjudicated in the Supreme Court of the United States," *NAR*, V (May 1817), III; for detailed discussion of institutional sources of uncertainty in local law see *Forums of Order*, 52. For case law and its lack of uniformity see: *Fenoville v. Hamilton*, 35 Ala. 319 (1859); and *Bank of Mobile v. Hall*, 6 Ala. 639 (1844); *Becker v. Sandusky*, 1 Minn. 311 (1856) and *Rosmond v. Graham*, 54 Minn. 323 (1893); *Goodman v. Simonds*, 19 Mo. 106 (1853) *Grant v. Kidwell* 30 Mo. 455 (1860); *Exchange National Bank v. Coe*, 95 Ark. 387 (1910); *Atchison v. Davidson*, 2 Pin. 48 (1847) and *Cook v. Helms*, 5 Wis. 107 (1856); *Platt v. Eads*, 1 Blackf. 81 (1820) and *Elliott v. Armstrong*, 2 Bankf. 231 (1829). I am indebted to Morris S. Arnold, who brought the two Indiana cases to my attention. See also *Homes v. Smyth*, 16 Maine 177 (1839), and *Burch v. Scribner*, 11 Conn. 388 (1836) for case upholding the negotiability of bill received for preexisting debts; see *Riley and Van Amringo v. Johnson*, 8 Ohio 526 (1838), and *Carlise v. Wishart*, II Ohio 173 (1842) for oscillation on the point in this state; and Horwitz *Transformation*, 212–26; Story's *Commentaries on the Law of Promissory Notes*, 3, 41, 44, 49, 128, 190, 194, 268–70, 423. A remarkable survey of each state in 1822, which supports the interpretation

here, is William Griffith, *Annual Law Register of the United States* (only vols. III and IV were published, Burlington, 1822), III: 22, 24, 48, 78–79, 118, 142–143, 224–225, 227, 264, 268–69, 362, 365, 403–04, 424, 445, 447, 468, 518–19, 521; IV: 587, 627–628, 670–71, 796, 801, 864, 866, 943, 946, 1006, 1008, 1065, 1071, 1141, 1144, 1300.

34. *The History of Land Titles in Massachusetts* (Boston, 1801), 353. "Remarks Upon Uniformity in Commercial Law," *United States Commercial & Statistical Register* I (July 1839), 53–55.

35. William H. DeForest, "Trial by Jury in Commercial Cases," *Hunt's* XXXV (September 1856), 303.

36. For the English background see S. F. C. Milsom, *Historical Foundations of the Common Law* (London, 1969), 74–87, 181–82. Gulian C. Verplank, *Speech When in Committee of the Whole in the Senate of New York, on Several Bills and Resolutions for the Amendment of the Law and the Reform of the Judicial System* (Albany, 1839), 21; and Joseph Story, *Commentaries on Equity Jurisprudence as Administered in England and America* (Boston, 1835), 82–83, are good primary sources on this matter. See also Lawrence M. Friedman, *A History of American Law* (New York, 1973), 47–48, 130–131, 346–147.

37. Edward S. Corwin, "The Progress of Constitutional Theory between the Declaration of Independence and the Meeting of the Philadelphia Convention," *American Historical Review*, XXX (April, 1925), 511–36; Allan Nevins, *The American States during and after the Revolution, 1775–1789* (New York, 1969), 454; Arndt M. Stickles, *The Critical Court Struggle in Kentucky, 1819–1929* (Bloomington, 1929); Robert F. Faulkner, *The Jurisprudence of John Marshall* (Princeton, 1968, 70–74; Peter J. Coleman, *Debtors and Creditors in America: Insolvency, Imprisonment for Debt, and Bankruptcy, 1607–1900* (Madison, 1974), 278–279.

38. Samuel Rezneck, "The Depression of 1819–1822, A Social History," *The American Historical Review* XXXIX (October 1933), 43–46; *Bank of Augusta* v. *Earle*, 13 Peters 519 (1839); James Kent, "The Law of Corporation: Chancellor Kent's Opinion," *The Law Reporter* I (July 1838), 58; "Mercantile Law," *Hunt's* I (December 1839), 511–12; Carl B. Swisher, *Roger B. Taney* (Hamden, 1961), 380–86. For discussion of Kentucky's duplicate court system see *Forums of Order*, 22–23, 27–28, and sources cited there.

39. "Commercial Lawyers," *Hunt's* XIV (January 1846), 64, 65–66.

40. J. K. Angell, "Elements of Commercial Law," *Hunt's* XV (August 1846), 137, 134–35. *Robinson* v. *Jones* 8 Mass. 536 (1812); see also Upton, "Law of Debtor and Creditor," *Hunt's* XV (July 1846), 70–71, and *Blackstone's Commentaries: With Notes of Reference to the Constitution and Laws of the United States and Commonwealth of Virginia* (St. George Tucker ed., Philadelphia, 1803), 430; John Milton Goodenow, *Historical Sketches of the Principles and Maxims of American Jurisprudence in Contrast with the Doctrines of the English Common Law on the Subject of Crimes and Punishments* (Steubenville, 1819), 36. Francis Hilliard, *The Elements of Law* (Boston, 1835), 106; Sullivan, *Land Titles*, 352; Richard Sulley, "True Theory of Capital and Labor," *Hunt's* XX (April 1849), 370; William Kent, "The Law of Nations," *Hunt's* I (August 1839), 99; "Law of Debtor and Creditor in Iowa," *Hunt's* VII (November 1842), 429; Thomas G. Fessenden, *An Essay on the Law of Patents for New Inventions* (Boston, 1810), 42. Robert W. and Alexander J. Carlyle, *A History of Mediaval Political Theory in the West* (London, 1903), 61; "Mercantile Law," *Hunt's* I (January 1839), 66.

41. "Sergent's Reports," *North American Review* XXI (October 1825), 380. David

R. Jacques, "Mercantile Law for Merchants—Smith's Compendium of Mercantile Law," *Hunt's* XVIII (August 1847), 164–65.

42. *Commentaries on American Law*, 4 vols. (12th ed., 1873), 477. "Common Law," *NAR* XIX (October 1824), 420.

43. For uncertainty concerning the conception of law see Perry Miller, *The Life of the Mind in America From the Revolution to the Civil War* (New York, 1965), 159. Hoffman, *A Course of Legal Study*, 2 vols. (2d. ed., Baltimore, 1836), 416. William Sampson, "On the Common Law," *NAR*, XIX, (October 1824), 427.

44. Tucker, *Blackstone's Commentaries*, 380. See note 3 for discussion of federal common law of crimes. For *Wheaton v. Peters*, 8 Peters 591 (1834) see Maurice G. Baxter, *Daniel Webster and the Supreme Court* (Amherst, 1966), 147–53; William W. Crosskey, *Politics and the Constitution in the History of the United States*, 2 vols. (Chicago, 1953), II, 447–80, 486.

45. 8 Peters 687; Baldwin, *A General View of the Oorigin and Nature of the Constitution and Government of the United States* (Philadelphia, 1837); see also "Common Law Jurisdiction," *NAR*, XXI (July, 1825), 104–141.

46. *U.S.* v. *Crosby*, 7 Cranch 115 (1812); *Jackson c. Chew*, 12 Wheaton 153 (1827); *Green v. Neal*, 6 Peters 291 (1832).

47. 8 Wheaton, 502.

48. *Robinson v. Campbell* 3 Wheaton 212 (1818); Kent, *Commentaries*, I, 213; *Wayman v. Southard*, 10 Wheaton 1 (1825). Circuit opinions includes: *Golden v. Prince*, 10 Fed. Cases 542 (CCD Penn., 1814); *Campbell v. Claudius*, 4 Fed. Cases 1161 (CCD Penn., 1817); *Brewster v. Gelston*, 4 Fed. Cases, 82 (CCDNY, 1825); *Lane v. Townsend*, 14 Fed. Cases 1087 (CCD Maine, 1835).

49. *Ingraham v. Gibbs*, 2 Dallas 136 (1791); *Clarke v. Russel*, 3 Dallas 424 (1799); *Brown v. Berry*, 3 Dallas 368 (1797); *Ludlow v. Bingham*, 4 Dallas 44 (1799). For comment on the BUS decisions see Goebel, *Antecedents*, 655. *Brown v. Van Braam*, 3 Dallas 350 (1797).

50. 3 Dallas 356.

51. *Dunlope v. Silver*, 8 Fed. Cases 92 (CCDC, 1801); *Riddle v. Mandeville*, 20 Fed. Cases 756 (CCDC, 1802) were the circuit cases. *Mandeville v. Riddle* 1 Cranch 290 (1803) overruled the latter of these; the decision which used equity to uphold the original position of the circuit court was *Riddle and Co. v. Mandeville and Jamesson*, 5 Cranch 32–33 (1809). See also footnote in *Harris v. Johnston*, 3 Cranch 316 (1806). I am indebted to Morton J. Horwitz for these citations. *Collidge v. Payson*, 2 Wheaton 75 (1817). See also *Payson v. Coolidge*, 19 Fed. Cases 19 (CCD, Mass., 1814 and *Townsley v. Sumrall*, 2 Peters 182 (1829).

52. 28 Fed. Cases 1065 (CCDRI, 1812).

53. Ibid.

54. *Clark's Executors v. Van Reimsdyk*, 9 Cranch 148 (1815). Julius Goebel, Jr., "The Common Law and the Constitution," in W. M. Jones, ed. *Chief Justice John Marshall: A Reappraisal* (Ithaca, 1956), 101–123.

55. *William v. Suffolk Ins. Co.*, 29 Fed. Cases 1405 (CCD Mass., 1838); see also *Donnell v. Columbian Ins. Co.*, 7 Fed. Cases 889 (CCD Mass., 1836); *Robinson v. Common Wealth Ins. Co.* 20 Fed. Cases, 1002 (CCD Mass., 1839).

56. *Riley v. Anderson*, 20 Fed. Cases 802 (CCD Ohio, 1841); the Ohio case was *Riley and Van Amringo v. Johnson*, 8 Ohio 526 (1838).

57. Sullivan, *Land Titles*, 52; Tucker, *Blackstone's Commentaries*, 430; Du Ponceau, *A Dissertation*, 39, 41, 119; William Rawle, *A View of the Constitution of the United*

States (Philadelphia, 1829), 225; Sergeant, *Constitutional Law*, 148–150. See also Baldwin, *General View*, 3, 7; and William Alexander Duer, *A Course of Lectures on the Constitution of the United States* (New York, 1852), 185–86.

58. Frank, *Daniel Dissenting*, 183, 184, 281. See also for general states' rights support for creditor rights and the role of the federal courts in enforcing them: Curtis Nettles, "The Mississippi Valley and the Federal Judiciary, 1807–1837," *The Mississippi Valley Historical Review* XII (1925), 202–26; Van Buren to Jackson, November 12, 1834, in *The Correspondence of Andrew Jackson*, 6 vols. (John Spencer Basset ed., New York, 1969), III, 167.

59. For detailed analysis of Catron's ground for concurring see *Forums of Order*, 9–10, 38–39, 80–81.

60. Joseph Story, *Commentaries on the Conflict of Laws, Foreign and Domestic in Regard to Marriages, Divorces, Wills, Successions, and Judgments* (Boston, 1834), 526–527, 7, 8, 56.

61. Ibid., 25, 33, 34, 37. For contrary views see Crosskey, *Politics and the Constitution*, I, 36, 555, 569, 573–574; Horwitz, *American Law*, 247–249.

62. 13 Peters 589 (1839).

63. For fuller discussion of the relationship between commercial law and sharp practices see *Forums of Order*, 1–18, 36–42, 53–68.

64. See note 24.

65. See *Forums of Order*, 82–76 for basic continuities in the business background of the Supreme Court in 1842. See also notes 5, 40, and 63.

CHAPTER II

1. 16 Peters 495.

2. *Carlise* v. *Wisehart*, 11 Ohio 191–92 (1842). See Chapter 1 for discussion of the earlier Ohio decision.

3. *Stalker* v. *McDonald*, 6 Hill 93 (1843); *Bank of Mobile* v. *Hall*, 6 Ala. 639 (1844); *Bostwick* v. *Dodge*, 1 Douglass 413 (1844); *Reddick* v. *Jones*, 6 Iredell's Law 107 (1847); *Allaire* v. *Hartshorne*, 1 Zabriske 665 (1847); *Blanchard* v. *Stevens*, 3 Cushing 162 (1849). James Kent, *Commentaries On American Law* (4 vols., 6 ed., New York, 1845), III, 80.

4. J. I. C. Hare and H. B. Wallace, eds., *American Leading Cases*, 2 vols. (2d. ed., Philadelphia, 1851), 344; Theophilus Parsons, *The Elements of Mercantile Law* (2d. ed., Boston, 1862), 151; Parsons, *A Treatise on the Law of Promissory Notes and Bills of Exchange*, 2 vols. (2d. ed., Boston, 1876), I, 221–23, II, 43; Parsons, *The Personal and Property Rights of a Citizen of the United States* (Hartford, 1877), 72–73, 641–43; "Leading Cases Upon Commercial Law," *Hunt's Merchants' Magazine* XVII (November 1847), 504; John William Wallace, *The Want of Uniformity in the Commercial Law Between the Different States of our Union: A Discourse* (Philadelphia, 1851), 32.

5. *Lane* v. *Vick*, 3 Howard 477, 481–82 (1845); *Daley's Lessee* v. *James*, 8 Wheaton 542 (1823).

6. 5 Howard 134 (1847); see also *Groves* v. *Slaughter* 15 Peters 449 (1841), and Carl B. Swisher, *The Taney Period 1836–64, History of the United States Supreme Court*, 11 vols. (Paul Freund ed., New York, 1974), V, 334–35.

7. Ibid.; 5 Howard 139 (1847).

8. *Williamson* v. *Berry,* 8 How. 495, 565 (1850); *Withers* v. *Greene,* 8 Howard 213 (1850). Swisher, *Taney Period,* 333; Morton J. Horwitz, *The Transformation of American Law* (Cambridge, 1977), 224–26.

9. *Meade* v. *Beale,* 16 Fed Cas. 1283 (C.C.D. Maryland, 1850); *Pease* v. *Peck,* 18 How. 595 (1855).

10. *Beauregard* v. *The City of New Orleans,* 18 How. 497, 507 (1855); *Dodge* v. *Woolsey,* 18 How. 371 (1855); *Suydom* v. *Williamson,* 24 How. 427 (1860).

11. 18 Howard 517, 521 (1847). Horwitz, *American Law,* 225–26, 341.

12. G. Edward White, *The American Judicial Tradition: Profiles of Leading American Judges* (New York, 1976) 64–83, especially, 72–74.

13. Ibid.

14. Ibid., 70–71; Swisher, *Taney Period,* 128–154, 332–333.

15. Lawrence Friedman, *A History of American Law* (New York, 1972), 337; *Ex parte Schollenberger,* 96 U.S. 369 (1877); Tony Freyer, *Forums of Order: Federal Courts and Business in American History* (Greenwich, 1979), Ch. VI, note 58.

16. *Monthly Western Jurist,* II (September 1875), 312–13.

17. *Galpin* v. *Page,* 9 Fed. Cas. 1131, 1135 (C.C.D. Calif., 1874). Also: *Bradley* v. *Lill,* 3 Fed. Cas. 1155 (CCND Ill., 1861); *Burt* v. *Keyes,* 4 Fed. Cas. 858 (CCND Ohio, 1861).

18. 10 Wallace 497, 504, 506 (1870).

19. George C. Holt, *The Concurrent Jurisdiction of the Federal and State Courts* (New York, 1888), 180–181.

20. *Gelpcke* v. *City of Dubuque,* 1 Wall. 175 (1864). *Dubuque Co.* v. *Dubuque & Pacific R.R. Co.,* 4 Green 1 (1853); *Clapp* v. *Cedar Co.,* 5 Ia. 15 (1857); *Ring* v. *County of Johnson,* 6 Ia. 265 (1858); *State* v. *Board of Equalization of the County of Johnson,* 10 Ia. 157 (1859) and other cases supported the localities bond schemes. *Burlington & Missouri R.R. Co.* v. *County of Wapello,* 13 Ia. 388 (1862) overruled these precedents. Carter Goodrich, *Government Promotion of American Canals and Railroads* (New York, 1960), 80, 141–149, 158 f. 212 ff., 216 f. 222 f., 230–260 and Charles Fairman, *Reconstruction and Reunion, 1864–88: History of the Supreme Court of the United States,* 11 vols. (New York, 1971), VI, P.T. 1, 918–1116 discuss local resistance. See also Mitchell Wendell, *Relations between the Federal and State Courts* (New York, 1949), 162–65; Freyer, *Forums of Order,* Ch. VI, VII.

21. 1 Wallace 175, 200.

22. Ibid., 201. See also Fairman, *Reconstruction and Reunion,* 939, for an analysis of the destinction between "general law" and "independent judgment."

23. William Gillette, "Samuel Miller," *The Justices of the United States Supreme Court, 1789–1969: Their Lives and Major Opinions* (Leon Friedman and Fred L. Israel eds., New York, 1969), 1019–1020. See also Charles Fairman, *Mr. Justice Miller and the Supreme Court, 1862–1900* (Cambridge, 1939), 213–21; *Butz* v. *City of Muscatine,* 8 Wallace 587 (1869).

24. Charles Warren, *The Supreme Court in United States History,* 3 vols. (Cambridge, 1923), II, 532, gives a state by state breakdown of cases. Goodrich, *Government Promotion,* 230–262 has financial estimates. Freyer, *Forums of Order,* Ch. VI, notes 22 and 23, deals with extent of local resistance; and Wendell, *Relations,* 160.

25. *People* v. *Salem,* 20 Mich. 452 (1870); *Whiting* v. *Sheboygan and Fond du Lac R.R. Co.,* 25 Wis. 167 (1870) were other state cases upholding repudiations. The Court let stand repudiations in *Fairfield* v. *Gallatin County,* 100 U.S. 47 (1879) and *Town of South Ottawa* v. *Perkins,* 94 U.S. 260 (1876). For the Court's usual treatment of the

issue see: *Town of Venice* v. *Murdock,* 92 U.S. 494, 501 (1875); *Town of Coloma* v. *Eaves* 92 U.S. 484 (1875).

26. See the *Murdock* case 92 U.S. 502 for Miller, Field, and Davis dissents. *Burgess* v. *Seligman* 107 U.S. 20 (1882).

27. *Chamberlain* v. *Mil. & Miss. R.R. Co.,* 11 Wis. 239 (1860); *Farwell* v. *R.R. Co.* 4 Met. 49 (1850); *Ryan* v. *The Chicago & Northwestern R.R. Co.,* 60 Ill. 171 (1871); *Flike* v. *The Boston & Albany Co.,* 53 N.Y. Rep. 549 (1873); *Mullan* v. *Philadelphia & Southern Mail Steamship Co.,* 78 Pa. St. 25 (1875); *Whalen* v. *The Centenary Church of St. Louis,* 62 Mo. 327 (1876); *Chicago & Northwestern R.R. Co.* v. *Bayfield* 37 Mich. 205 (1877); *Cowles* v. *Richmond & Danville R.R. Co.,* 84 N. Car. 309 (1881). *Davis* v. *Central Vermont R.R. Co.,* 55 Vt. 84 (1882); *Moore* v. *The Wabash, St. Louis & Pacific R.R. Co.,* 85 Mo. 588 (1885). Thomas G. Shearman and Amasa A. Redfield, *A Treatise on the Law of Negligence,* 2 vols. (4th ed., New York, 1888), I, 1–24, 61–70, 230–249. Robert S. Hunt, *Law and Locomotives: The Impact of the Railroad on Wisconsin Law in the Nineteenth Century* (Madison, 1958), 151–157.

28. *Central Law Journal,* X (Jan. 1880), 17; Freyer, *Forums of Order,* Ch. VI, note 25.

29. *Howard and Wife* v. *Denver & R.G. Ry. Co.,* 26 Fed. Rep. 837, 843 (CCD Colorado, 1886). For drift of opinion see *Chicago* v. *Robbins,* 2 Black, 418 (1862); *Railroad Company* v. *Lockwood,* 17 Wallace 357 (1873); *Buckley* v. *Gould & Curry Silver Mining Co.,* 14 Fed. Rep. 833 (CCD Nev., 1882); *Randall* v. *Baltimore and Ohio R.R. Co.,* 109 U.S. 478 (1883); *Chicago, Milwaukee & St. Paul R. Co.* v. *Ross,* 112 U.S. 787 (1884); *Garrahy* v. *Kansas City, St. J. & C.B.R. Co.,* 25 Fed. Rep. 258 (CCD Kansas, 1885); *Quinn* v. *New Jersey Lighterage Co.,* 23 Fed. Rep. 363 (CCEDNY, 1885); *Little* v. *Hackett,* 116 U.S. 366 (1886); *Van Wickle* v. *Manhattan Ry. Co.,* 32 Fed. Rep. 278 (CCSDNY, 1886); *Easton* v. *Houston & T.C. Ry. Co.,* 32 Fed. Rep. 893 (CCED Tex, 1887); *Anderson* v. *Winston,* 31 Fed. Rep. 528 (CCD Minn., 1887); *McCrory, Adm'x* v. *Chicago, M. & St. P. Ry. Co.,* 31 Fed. Rep. (CCD Minn., 1887); *Van Avery* v. *Union Pac. Ry. Co.,* 35 Fed. Rep. 40 (CCD Colorado, 1888); *Heckman* v. *Mackey,* 35 Fed. Rep. 353 (CCSDNY, 1888); *Hardy* v. *Minneapolis & St. L. Ry. Co.,* 36 Fed. Rep. 657 (CCD Minn., 1888); *Ragsdale* v. *Northern Pac. R. Co.,* 42 Fed. Rep. 383 (CCD Minn., 1889); *Borgman* v. *Omaha & St. Louis Ry. Co.,* 41 Fed. Rep. 667 (CCSD Iowa, 1890); *Atchison, T & S.F.R. Co.* v. *Wilson,* 48 Fed. Rep. 57 (CCA, 8th, 1891); *Woods* v. *Lindall,* 48 Fed. Rep. 62 (CCA, 8th, 1891); *Northern Pac. R. Co.* v. *Peterson,* 51 Fed. Rep. 182 (CCA 8th, 1892); *B & O R.R. Co.* v. *Baugh,* 149 U.S. 368 (1892).

30. 2 Black. 418.

31. 112 U.S. 794. See *Little* v. *Hackett* 116 U.S. 366 (1886) by-stander case; *Buckley* case 14 Fed. Rep. 833 (CCD Nev., 1882) and *Randall* 109 U.S. 478 (1883) are examples of unwillingness to extend protection in fellow-servant cases to employees.

32. The *Garrahy* case, 25 Fed. Rep. 258 (CCD Kan., 1885). See note 29 for other cases.

33. Ibid., 265–266.

34. The *Howard Case,* 26 Fed. Rep. 837, 843, 845 (CCD Colorado, 1886) expressed Brewer's views on *Ross.* The *Borgman* cite is 41 Fed. Rep. 667, 668, 670–671 (CCSD Iowa, 1890).

35. *Bucher* v. *Cheshire R.R. Co.,* 125 U.S. 555 (1887).

36. Ibid., 583–584, 585.

37. 147 U.S. 101 (1893); 149 U.S. 368.

38. *Baugh,* 149 U.S. 368, 370, 373.

39. Ibid., 379, 398.

40. Ibid., 399, 397, 403, 407, 408–09, 411.

41. Ibid., 395, 403. Apparantly, Field's dissent was motivated primarily by anger over the majority's refusal to apply his *Ross* opinion in the *Baugh* case. He hated the fellow-servant rule; his attack on the constitutional dimension of the concept of general law should not, therefore, be considered a statement of reasoned jurisprudential theory, but rather a tactical maneuver designed to undermine the logic of Brewer's opinion. I am indebted to Charles McCurdy, Field's most recent biographer, for this insight.

42. *Swift* v. *Philadelphia & R.R. Co.*, 64 Fed. Rep. 59 (C.C.N.D. Ill., 1894). See White, *Judicial Tradition*, 146–149.

43. See Chapter 1 for the antebellum side of this story.

44. *Byrne* v. *Kansas City, FT. S. & M.R. Co.*, 61 Fed. Rep. 605, 614 (CCA 6th, 1894). *Murray* v. *Chicago & N.W. Ry. Co.*, 62 Fed. Rep. 24, 25 (C.C.N.D. Iowa, 1894).

45. Charles Warren, "Corporations and Diversity Citizenship," XIX *University of Virginia Law Review* (May 1933), 661–689. See also discussion of Meigs and Hare below.

46. *Railroad and Corporation Law Journal*, I (Jan. 1887), 26–27.

47. *Central Law Journal* XVIII (April, 1884), 281–82. See Freyer, *Forums of Order*, Ch. VIII, for fuller discussion.

48. Thomas C. Cochran, *Railroad Leaders, 1845–1890: The Business Mind in Action* (Cambridge, 1953), 184–85.

49. As quoted, Edward Chase Kirkland, *Men, Cities, and Transportation: A Study in New England History, 1820–1900* (Cambridge, 1918), 19.

50. Robert D. Marcus, *Grand Old Party: Political Structure in the Gilded Age, 1880–1896* (New York, 1971), 50–53, 153, 195, 256, 263.

51. Edward Chase Kirkland, *Dream and Thought in the Business Community, 1860–1900* (Ithaca, 1956), 135. See also Thomas C. Cochran, *Business in American Life: A History* (New York, 1972), 194–195.

52. Freyer, *Forums of Order*, Ch. VI, VII. Alfred D. Chandler, Jr., *The Visible Hand: The Managerial Revolution in American Business* (Cambridge, 1977) and Robert Wiebe, *The Search for Order: 1877–1920*.

53. See note 45; Felix Frankfurter and James M. Landis, *The Business of the Supreme Court: A Study in the Federal Judicial System* (New York, 1928), 85–100; Freyer, *Forums of Order*, Ch. VII.

54. Ibid. 10 *Congressional Record*, Pt. 1, 2nd. Sess. 820. During the debates over the Culberson Bill petitions from St. Louis, Cincinnati, Akron, and Toledo came to Congress against the bill. See: "Goodbar, White & Co., Tennent, Walker, and other businessmen and merchants of Saint Louis, Mo.," 15 *Cong. Rec.*, Part 5, 1st Sess. (1884), 5171; Board of Trade & Transportation of the City of Cincinnati," 15 *Cong. Rec.*, Part 5, 1st Sess. (1884), 5378; "Large number of businessmen, lawyers, and others in Toledo, Ohio," 15 *Cong. Rec.*, Part 5, 1st Sess. (1884), 5469; "Diamond Match Co.," of Akron, Ohio," 15 *Cong. Rec.*, Part 5, 1st Sess. (1884), 5513; "John Shillito Co.," 15 *Cong. Rec.*, Part 5, 1st Sess. (1884), 5611.

55. 10 *Cong. Rec.*, Part 1, 2nd Sess. (1880), 724.

56. 10 *Cong. Rec.*, Part 1, 2nd Sess. (1880), 1278.

57. 13 *Cong. Rec.*, Part 4, 1st Sess. (1882), 336–37.

58. 14 *Cong. Rec.*, Part 2, 2nd Sess. (1883), 1248, 1246.

174 *Notes*

59. *Central Law Journal* XXI (December 1885), 518. Warren, "Corporations and Diversity," 681. Freyer, *Forums of Order,* Ch. VII.

60. *Central Law Journal* XXV (September 1887), 241–42. Frankfurter and Landis, *Supreme Court,* 101.

61. Edward McCrady, "Reorganization of the Federal Courts," *Central Law Journal* III (May 1876), 311; *Majority and Minority Reports . . . on the Remedy for Delays . . . The Debate of the American Bar Association* (Philadelphia, 1882), 27, 40–41.

62. *Constitutional History of the United States as seen in the Development of American Law* (New York, 1889), 253, 259, 260–268, 274–278.

63. Ibid., 280–281.

64. W. H. Taft, "Criticism of the Federal Judiciary," *American Law Review* XXIX (September–October 1895), 651. Articles defending *Swift:* Percy Werner, "National Common Law: On the Introduction and Modification of the Common Law in the United States," *Southern Law Review* VIII (December 1882), 414–31; Conrad Reno, "Impairment of Contracts by change of Judicial Opinions," *American Law Review* XXIII (March–April, 1889), 195–96. Treatises: Holt, *Concurrent Jurisdiction* (New York, 1888); Benjamin R. Curtis, *Peculiar Jurisprudence of the Courts of the United States* (Boston, 1880), 200–212; Amos M. Thayer, *Jurisdiction of the Federal Courts* (St. Louis, 1895), 48; Thomas M. Cooley, *The General Principles of the Constitutional Law in the United States of America* (Boston, 1898), 151.

65. Robert G. Street, "Is There a General Commercial Law Administered by the Courts of the United States?" *The American Law Register* XXI (August 1873), 473–481; William B. Hornblower, "Conflict Between Federal and State Decisions," *American Law Review,* XIV (March 1880), 211–228; J. B. Heiskell, *Conflict between Federal and State Decisions American Law Review* XVI (October 1882), 743–760; William M. Meigs, "Decisions of the Federal Courts on Questions of State Law," *Southern Law Review* VIII (December 1882), 452–493; J. B. Heiskell, "Retrospective Decisions," *American Law Review* XXII (July–August 1888), 523–537; W. M. Meigs, "Shall the State Courts adopt the Federal Doctrine of 'General Principles of Jurisprudence?' " *Central Law Journal* XXIX (December 1889), 465–470, 485–490; William H. Rand, Jr., *"Swift* v. *Tyson* versus *Gelpke* v. *Dubuque,"* *Harvard Law Review* VIII (January 1895), 328–351.

66. Meigs, "General Principles of Jurisprudence," *Central Law Journal* XXIV (December 1889), 489.

67. Ibid., 467, 68, 85–87, 88.

68. Ibid., 465–470, 485–90. See also Meig's, "The Relief of the Supreme Court of the United States," *American Law Register* XXIII (June 1884), 360–70. For more general views see, *The Relation of the Judiciary to the Constitution* (New York, 1929), originally published 1885.

69. Kent, *Commentaries,* 4 vols. (12th ed., Boston, 1873), I, *419, n. 1 (a) and *342 n.l. For Holmes' early views on conflict of law see Stephen M. Boyd, "Mr. Justice Holmes and the Conflict of Laws, 1864–1902" (unpublished mss., 1958), located in O.W.H., Jr. papers, Harvard Law School, Paige Box #11 (used with author's permission).

70. *"Gelpcke* v. *Dubuque;* Federal and State Decisions," *Legal Essays* (Boston 1908), 146.

71. Ibid., 146, 148, 149; see also Arthur E. Sutherland, *The Law at Harvard: A History of Ideas and Men, 1817–1967* (Cambridge, 1967), 209–210. For the lecture notes see T. R. Powell "Notes taken from Gray's Lecture's on Constitutional Law, based on Thayer's Textbook, 1903–04," 393; Joseph H. Beale, "Notes on Thayer's

Constitutional Law Class, 1886" (no pagination); Moses Day Kimball, "Notes of J. B. Thayer's Lectures on Constitutional Law, 1891–92" 378, 381–382; Clarence Bunder, "Notes of Lectures on Constitutional Law, given by James Bradley Thayer, 1891–92," 21, 134. These notebooks are located in the manuscript division of Harvard Law School.

72. For the reference to the Pow Wow moot argument I am indebted to Mrs. Erika Chadbourn who pointed it out in "In Pow Wow, 1875–76," a box of moot arguments, located in the manuscript division of Harvard Law School. See also Paul Freund, *Mr. Justice Brandeis: A Centennial Memoir* (Typed script, HLS Lib, 1956), 1.

73. Wharton, *Commentaries on Law* (Philadelphia, 1884), 602–16. Hare, *American Constitutional Law*, 2 vols. (Boston, 1884); *The Law of Contracts* (Boston, 1887).

74. Hare, *Constitutional Law*, 1–3, vi–vii, 446–51, 530–531, 696–697, 726–727, 1107–1119.

75. Ibid., 1118, 1119.

76. Henry M. Hoyt, Jr., "Notes in John I. C. Hare Law Lectures, University of Pennsylvania, Session 1879–80," 137 (in Treasure Room, HLS). I am indebted to Miss Edith Henderson for this cite. Pepper discussed Hare's influence in his autobiography, *Philadelphia Lawyer: An Autobiography* (Philadelphia, 1944), 52.

77. *The Border Land of Federal and State Decisions* (Philadelphia, 1889). Miller's letter appears in Pepper's autobiography, 52–53.

78. Morton Keller, *Affairs of State: Public Life in Late Nineteenth Century America* (Cambridge, 1977), 1–33, 343–70.

79. Fred. Perry Powers, "Recent Centralizing Tendencies in the Supreme Court," *Political Science Quarterly* V (September 1890), 410. Powers is discussing commerce decisions here. In my *Forums of Order* Ch. VI and VII I attempt to show the connection between the *Swift* doctrine and the commerce, due process, and antitrust cases.

80. Ibid., notes 52, and 78 for nationalization of business. Quote from Hare, *Constitutional Law*, 450.

81. "Some Reflections on the Bar, its Integrity and Independence," *American Law Review* XXII (March–April, 1888), 178–179, 180. Arnold M. Paul, *Conservative Crisis on the Rule of Law: Attitudes on Bar and Bench, 1887–1895* (Ithaca, 1960) is an excellent treatment of this issue.

82. Dougherty "Reflections," *ALR*, XXII (March–April, 1888), 197.

83. Note 64.

84. Keller's analysis of the impact of the War on contemporaries' minds seems convincing here. It is perhaps useful to note that the war and the problems of federalism it spawned were the dominant events in the lives of the two generations who were critics of *Swift*. Born early in the century in 1816, Thayer and Hare faced the War and its aftermath during their most productive mature years. Meigs, Holmes, Brandeis, and Pepper, born at mid-century in 1852, 1841, 1856, 1867, struggled with the new order arising after the War, a fact which no doubt greatly influenced their views as they worked during their years of professional leadership in the first third of the twentieth century.

85. Ezra R. Thayer, "Judicial Legislation: Its Legitimate Function in the Development of the Common Law," *Harvard Law Review* V (November 1891), 172–201, especially, 177–178; Roscoe Pound, "Fifty Years of Jurisprudence," *Harvard Law Review* L (Feb. 1937), 557–582; Joseph H. Beale, Jr., "The Development of Jurisprudence During the Past Century," *Harvard Law Review* XVIII (September 1904), 271–83.

86. Ibid.; Chamberlain, *Constitutional History*, 283; James Bradley Thayer, "The

Teaching of English Law at Universities," *Legal Essays* (Boston, 1908), 367–87; Hare, *Law of Contracts*, 1–19; Wharton, *Commentaries*, iii–x; on Meigs see his articles cited above and his introduction to Brinton Coxe, *An Essay on Judicial Power and Unconstitutional Legislation* (Philadelphia, 1893); Pepper, *Borderland*, and *Autobiography*, 53.

87. Pepper, *Autobiography*, 51 and his *Legal Education and Admission to the Bar* (Philadelphia, 1895), 13–15. On Langdell see Grant Gilmore, *The Ages of American Law* (New Haven, 1977), 42, 43, 47; James Willard Hurst, *The Growth of American Law: The Law Makers* (Boston, 1950), 262–266, 68–71; Sutherland, *Law at Harvard*, 162–65, 174–178.

88. Notes 71, 76.

CHAPTER III

1. H. Parker Sharp and Joseph B. Brennan, "The Application of the Doctrine of *Swift* v. *Tyson* Since 1900," *Indiana Law Journal* IV (March 1929); 367–385 is an excellent overview of cases, including numerous citations to circuit court decisions. Felix Frankfurter, "Distribution of Judicial Power Between United States and State Courts," *Cornell Law Quarterly* XIII (June, 1928), 499–530, especially 523; Hessel E. Yntema and George H. Jaffin, "Preliminary Analysis of Concurrent Jurisdiction," *University of Pennsylvania Law Review* LXXIV (May 1931), 869–917; and reply Frankfurter, "A Note on Diversity Jurisdiction—In Reply to Professor Yntema," *University of Pennsylvania Law Review* LXXIV (May 1931), 1097–1100. Charles Warren, "Corporations and Diversity Citizenship," *Virginia Law Review* XIX (May 1933), 661–689, especially 686.

2. 197 U.S. 544, 573–74, 576 (1904). For comment see Thomas Dent, "The Common Law in Federal Jurisprudence," *Central Law Journal* LIX (August 1905), 123–134. The majority included McKenna, Harlan, Brewer, Brown, Day; minority, Fuller, White, Peckham, Holmes.

3. 215 U.S. 349, 271, 272. For comment see Henry Schofield, *"Swift* v. *Tyson:* Uniformity of Judge-made State Law in State and Federal Courts," *Illinois Law Review* IV (March 1910), 533–551; William M. Meigs, "Decisions of the Federal Courts on Questions of State Law," *American Law Review* XLV (January–February 1911), 47–77. The majority included Fuller, Harlan, Brewer, Day; minority, Holmes, White, McKenna.

4. 244 U.S. 205, 220, 222. This case generated difficult questions concerning admiralty and maritime jurisdiction. See, William J. Conlen, "Ten Years of the Jensen Case," *University of Pennsylvania Law Review* LXXVI (June 1928), 926–957. The dissenters in *Jensen* were Holmes, Brandeis, and Pitney (who wrote his own lengthy opinion).

5. 276 U.S. 518.

6. Ibid., 533, 35. This case raised much criticism and controversy. See below.

7. Senator Thomas J. Walsh, S. 4333, 69 *Cong. Rec.* 1st Sess. 1928, 7688; S. 96, 71 *Cong. Rec.,* 1st. Sess., 1929, 103. For the correspondence between Brandeis and Frankfurter, see: To Felix Frankfurter, April 10, 1928 Washington, D.C. 124½–25; to Felix Frankfurter, April 21, 1928, Washington, D.C., 125–125½, of manuscript

Letters of Louis D. Brandeis (Melvin I. Urofsky ed.), V. I am indebted to Professor Urofsky for this citation. I am indebted to Professor Robert Leflar for insight concerning the role of Chief Justice Taft involving efforts to end *Swift*. The citation for the letter is: Taft to Horace, June 12, 1928, Box 50, F. 23; Oliver Wendell Holmes, Jr., Papers Manuscript Division, HLS. Reference to the numerous articles in legal periodicals will be given below.

8. Merlo J. Pusey, *Charles Evans Hughes*, 2 vols. (New York, 1951), II, 710. *Brinkerhoff-Faris Co.* v. *Hill*, 281 U.S. 681 (1930); *Trainor Co.* v. *Aetna Casualty and Surety Co.*, 290 U.S. 47 (1933), *Mutual Life Ins. Co. of N.T.* v. *Johnson*, 293 U.S. 339 (1934); *Bosemann* v. *Connecticut General Life Ins. Co.*, 301 U.S. 196 (1937). See also *Burns Mortgage Co.* v. *Fried*, 292 U.S. 487 :1934), following the same course. But see *N.Y. Life Insurance Co.* v. *Gamer*, 303 U.S. 161 (1938).

9. See Chapter 2 for discussion.

10. *Holmes-Pollock Letters: The Correspondence of Mr. Justice Holmes and Sir Frederick Pollock 1874–1932*, 2 vols. Mark De Wolfe Howe ed., Cambridge, 1941), i, 157–158; ii, 53, 214–215. See also Pollock's reply in the latter reference, which develops a theory very similar to Thayer's, discussed above.

11. *Holmes-Laski Letters: The Correspondence of Mr. Justice Holmes and Harold J. Laski, 1916–1935*, 2 vols. Mark De Wolfe Howe ed., Cambridge, 1953), ii, 822–23, 1027, 1159.

12. Needham C. Collier, "State Laws in Federal Courts," *Central Law Journal* LVII (August 1903), 151; "A Plea Against Jurisdiction For Diversity of Citizenship," *CLJ* LXXVI (April, 1913), 266–267. See Ch. 2 for discussion of Culberson bill.

13. Collier, "Diversity of Citizenship," *CLJ* LXXVI (April, 1913), 267.

14. 70 *Cong. Rec.*, 1st Session, Sen. Rept., No. 626, (May 1928), 3; 71 *Cong. Rec.*, 2d. Sess., Sen. Rept., 691 (May 20, 1930), 5. See also Sharp and Brennan *"Swift* v. *Tyson,"* *Ind. L. J.*, IV (March 1929), 385. John J. Parker, "The Federal Jurisdiction and Recent Attacks Upon It," *American Bar Association Journal* XVIII (June 1932), 436–439; Robert C. Brown, "Jurisdiction of the Federal Courts Based on Diversity of Citizenship," *University of Pennsylvania Law Review* LXXVIII (December 1929), 189–192.

15. Hiram Johnson was successful, after several defeats in getting reform of diversity in cases involving utility commissions. See 72 *Cong. Rec.* 157. Sess., Sen. (1932), 12303–04; 72 *Cong. Rec.*, 1st. Sess., Sen. (1932), 13827–28. I am indebted to Professor Robert Leflar for information concerning localism in rural communities. See also Parker, "Federal Jurisdiction," *ABAJ*, XVIII (1932), 434; Brown, "Diversity of Citizenship," *Un. Pa. L. Rev.*, LXXVIII (December 1929), 179, 182–183, 188–190.

16. Parker, "Federal Jurisdiction," *ABAJ* XVIII (1932), 437, 438.

17. Hearings Before The Subcommittee on Improvements in Judicial Machinery of the Committee on the Judiciary United States Senate, 92 Congress, 1st Sess., S. 1876 (Washington, 1972), Part 1, 195–96; Brown, "Diversity of Citizenship," *Un. Pa. L. Rev.*, LXXVIII (December 1929), 182–183, 193.

18. Raymond T. Johnson, "State Law and the Federal Courts," *Kentucky Law Journal* XVII (May 1929), 366, 367.

19. Thomas W. Shelton, "Concurrent Jurisdiction—Its Necessity and Its Dangers," *Virginia Law Review* XV (December 1928), 144–45, 149–50; Armistead M. Dobie, "Seven Implications of Swift v. Tyson," *Vir. L. Rev.* XVI (January 1930), 238, 241.

20. *U.S. Statutes at Large,* I, 19. Charles Warren, "New Light on the Judiciary Act of 1789," *Harvard Law Review* XXXVI (November 1923), 82–87.

21. Holmes' cite, at 276 U.S. 532; Johnson, "State Law," *Ky. L. J.* XVII (May 1929), 361–362. Reference to Frankfurter's views: Frankfurter to Stone, May 9, 1938, p. 2, F.F. Papers Box 171, F17, Manuscript Division, HLS. Crosskey, *Politics and the Constitution,* II, 626–28, 866–71 argues persuasively that Warren misread the draft, a position concurred in by Henry J. Friendly, "In Praise of *Erie*—And of the new Federal Common Law," *New York University Law Review* XXXIX (May 1964), 389–90. See Chapter 1 for discussion of antebellum treatise writers whose analysis agrees with Crosskey.

22. Arthur E. Sutherland, "Material for Biography of Joseph Henry Beale," Paige Box # 15, manuscript division, HLS; "Sketches by distinguished HLS Graduates," dedicated to Beale," *Harvard Law Review* LVI (March 1943), 685–703.

23. Joseph H. Beale, "The Diversity of Laws," *The Colorado Bar Association* XIX (July 1916), 17–18, 22, 23; "The Development of Jurisprudence During the Past Century," *Harvard Law Review* XVIII (September 1905), 272, 283.

24. Joseph Henry Beale, *A Selection of Cases on the Conflict of Laws,* 2 vols. (Cambridge, 1928), I, 14–16; *A Selection of Cases on the Conflict of Laws,* 3 vols. (Cambridge, 1900), I, 95–117. For the notebooks see Manley O. Hudson, "Conflicts, J.H.B." (1909); Zechariah Chafee, Jr., "Conflict of Laws" (1912); Thomas R. Powell, "Conflict of Laws" (1904); Felix Frankfurter, "Conflict of Laws" (1900); Robert A. Leflar, "Conflict of Laws." These notebooks are located in the manuscript division, HLS.

25. Ibid.

26. Manley O. Hudson, "Seminar In Conflict of Laws, Beale" (1917); Joseph Henry Beale, "Reading Notes for Advanced Course in Conflict of Laws," Red Set, Harvard Law School Library.

27. John C. Gray, "Some Definitions and Questions in Jurisprudence," *Harvard Law Review* VI (April, 1892), 27; *The Nature and Sources of the Law* (New York, 1909), 254–259.

28. Gray, *Sources of Law,* 248–249, 253. See also Reed's notebook cited in Chapter 2.

29. Felix Frankfurter, "Distribution of Judicial Power Between United States and State Courts," *Cornell Law Quarterly* XIII (June 1928), 506, 515, 517–518, 520–525, 529–530. Frankfurter cited Warren and Gray with approval, though as we shall see, he did not think the former's scholarship conclusive.

30. Frankfurter to Holmes, September 9, 1928: in *Oliver Wendell Holmes Papers* 30–6. Manuscripts Division, HLS. See also letter from Frankfurter to Stone, May 9, 1938 Cambridge, Box 171, F17, FF, Manuscript Division, HLS. George E. Dane, "Notes on Federal Jurisdiction, Prof. Felix Frankfurter, Harvard Law School, 1927–28," manuscript division, HLS. I am indebted also to Professor Willard Hurst, Honorable Judge Henry J. Friendly, Professor Paul Freund, and Mr. Secretary W. Graham Claytor. Sharp and Brennan, "Application of *Swift* v. *Tyson,*" I.L.J., IV (March 1929), 367–385 had been a paper written for Frankfurter in 1928, when the two were students.

31. Frederick Green, "The Law as Precedent, Prophecy and Principles, State Decisions in Federal Courts," *Illinois Law Review* XIX (December 1924), 224; Hessel E. Yntema and George H. Jaffin. "Preliminary Analysis of Concurrent Jurisdiction," *University of Pennsylvania Law Review* LXXIX (May 1931) 869–917; Alton B. Parker, "The Common Law Jurisdiction of the United States Courts," *Yale Law Journal* XVII (November 1907), 1–20.

32. Arthur L. Corbin, "The Restatement of the Common Law by The American Law Institute," *Iowa Law Review* XV (1929), 25–26.

33. Ibid.

34. Ibid., 27, 35. See also Grant Gilmore, *The Ages of American Law* (New Haven, 1977), 78–80.

35. J. B. Fordham, "The Federal Courts and the Construction of Uniform State Laws," *North Carolina Law Review* VII (April 1929), 430. Memoranda, United States Supreme Court, Stone to Holmes, April 12, 1928, Washington, D.C. concerning tax-icab case, located in OWH Papers: OWH's bound set of his opinions, one vol. per Court Term, division, HLS. For material on Beale see notes 23–27. For reference to Brandeis' localism see Melvin I. Urofsky and David W. Levy, eds. *Letters of Louis D. Brandeis: Urban Reformer, 1870–1907,* 5 vols. (New York 1977), I, 114. I am indebted to Professor Paul Freund for this reference. The next citation concerning Brandeis is from Paul Freund *Mr. Justice Brandeis: A Centennial Memoir* (typed script, HLS Lib., 1956), 3; the reference to Brandeis views toward the Federal Rules of Civil Procedure was given to me by Professor Freund, a conclusion supported by *Preliminary Report on Efficiency in the Administration of Justice* (Boston 1914), esp. 18, 27–28.

36. *A Circular Letter Concerning the Administration of Justice* (Herbert Harley ed., Manistee, Michigan, 1912), 2, 13.

37. Charles I. Dawson, "Conflict of Decisions between State and Federal Courts in Kentucky and the Remedy," *Kentucky Law Journal* XX (November 1931), 4; *Efficiency in the Administration of Justice,* 28–29; Collier, "Diversity of Citizenship," CLJ, LXXVI (April, 1913), 263; Louis D. Brandeis, *Business—A Profession* (Boston 1914), 333–335, 337–341.

38. Oliver Wendell Holmes, *The Common Law* (Boston 1881), 5, 168, 244. M. D. Howe, "Holmes Seminar (April 19, 1961), Oliver Wendell Holmes, Jr., Papers, Manuscript Division, HLS. Carl M. Sapers, "Mr. Justice Holmes and the Road to Erie" (unpublished paper, 1958), Manuscript Division, HLS, used by permission of the author. See also Gilmore, *American Law,* 48–51, 67; Mark De Wolfe Howe, *Justice Oliver Wendell Holmes: The Proving Years, 1870–1882* (Cambridge, 1963) II.

39. Ibid., see notes 29–32.

40. The following narrative involving the facts and early stages of the Tompkins litigation follows closely Irving Younger, "What Happened in *Erie*" (manuscript, used by permission of the author). Where I quote directly, reference will be given to the page of the manuscript, otherwise no cite will be given.

41. *Falchetti* v. *Pennsylvania R.R. Co.,* 307 Pa. 203 (1932).

42. The decisions in the Federal District Court of Pennsylvania were: *Houston* v. *Delaware, L. & W.R.R. Co.,* 274 Fed. 599 (3d Cir. 1921); *Turk* v. *Neward Fire Ins. Co.,* 4 F. 2d. 56 (3d Cir. 1926); *Perucca* v. *Baltimore & O.R.R. Co.,* 35 F. 2d. 113 (3d. Cir. 1929); *Kehoe* v. *Central Park Amusement Co.,* 52 F. 2d. 916 (3d. Cir. 1931).

43. As quoted, Younger, "What Happened," 16.

44. Ibid., 16–18.

45. Ibid., 19.

46. Ibid., 21.

47. Ibid., 22.

48. Ibid., as quoted, 22.

49. 90 F. 2d. 604 (2d. Cir., 1937).

50. Interview, W. Graham Claytor, Jr., July 11, 1978.

51. Younger, "What Happened," 24–26.

52. Ibid., 26–27. Claytor interview, July 11, 1978.
53. Ibid., 28, 30–31.
54. Ibid., 32.
55. Pusey, *Hughes,* II, 710. The references to the drafts of the *Erie* opinion are contained in five folders marked 107-5 through 107-9 *Erie R.R.* v. *Tompkins* Oct. Term 1937, in the files of Mr. Justice Brandeis' Court papers located in Manuscripts Division, Harvard Law School. The drafts are rarely numbered, and included different combinations of handwritten and printed script. The drafting process culminated in two polished versions of the opinion: one marked March 28 and the other April 25, the version reported in 304 U.S. 64 (1938). The references below are to the folder in which the draft material is located. Where appropriate, I cite memoranda and either one or both of the March 28 and April 25 versions. The references to the positions of Reed and Black are cited below.
56. As quoted, Alpheus T. Mason, *Harlan Fiske Stone; Pillar of the Law* (New York, 1956), 478.
57. Claytor interview, July 11, 1978. Details of Justice Brandeis' procedure for preparing opinions are based on discussions with his former law clerks Professors Freund and Hurst, Honorable Judge Friendly, and Mr. Claytor.
58. 107-5.
59. Ibid.
60. Memoranda written by Mr. Claytor, "Pennsylvania Law," 1–2, 6 in 107-5.
61. These sources are discussed in Chapter 2, and above in this chapter.
62. 107-5.
63. Ibid.
64. Ibid.
65. 107-7 contains printed drafts, with corrections, deletions, and additions, for period March 19 through March 29 circulated among the members of the Court, to which Stone, Reed, and Black replied. In this copy Claytor inserted a number of changes concerning the Pennsylvania law. Claytor interview, July 11, 1978.
66. Reed to Brandeis, March 21, 1938 and March 23, 1938 in 107-7.
67. Brandeis to Reed, March 24, 1938, 107-7.
68. Reed to Brandeis, March 23, 1938 and draft of concurrence, 107-7.
69. Black to Brandeis, March 22, 1938, 107-7. See also Claytor, "Pennsylvania Law," 6.
70. Stone to Brandeis, March 23, 1938, 107-7. This letter and that cited in the next note are cited in Mason, *Stone,* 478, 479.
71. Stone to Brandeis, March 25, 1938, 107-7.
72. March 28 version, 107-7 compared with April 25 version 107-8. Compare Mason, *Stone,* 478, 479.
73. 107-8.
74. Ibid.
75. Ibid. The following citations are from an undated memorandum. This memorandum Brandeis prepared after receiving the draft of Butler's dissent. This memoranda is in 107-8.
76. Ibid.
77. 107-9. This file includes finished copies of the dissent and concurrence of Justices Butler and Reed and the copies of both the March 28 and April 25 versions of the majority opinion with notes of Justices Stone, Black, Roberts, and Chief Justice

Hughes. These were incorporated into 304 U.S. 63 (1938) as the decision of the Court, with concurrence and dissent (joined by Justice McReynolds).

78. *Tompkins* v. *Erie R.R. Co.,* 98 F. 2d 49 (2 Cir. 1938). Younger, "What Happened," 34–36, and for the citation to Judge Mandlebaum's "unique syntax," see note 37. I am indebted to Mr. Aaron Danzig for his recollections concerning this and other stages of the *Erie* litigation.

79. Warren to Brandeis, April 27, 1938; N. E. Snyder to Brandeis, May 13, 1938. Both in 107-9, LDB Court papers cited in note 55. Willard Hurst to Brandeis, May 19, 1938; also Robert Moschzisker to Brandeis, May 20, 1938 and Louis L. Jaffe, May 15, 1938; these three letters were located by Mrs. F. R. Hodgson, in the Brandeis papers, University Archives & Historical Research Center, University of Louisville. Robert H. Jackson, "The Rise and Fall of *Swift* v. *Tyson,*" *American Bar Association Journal* XXIV (May 1938), 609, 644. A. Hand to Frankfurter, May 10, 1938; Shulman to Frankfurter, May 21, 1938; Frankfurter to Stone May 9, 1938; these references are located in Box 198-F8, Box 171-F17, Frankfurter papers HLS.

80. Younger, "What Happened," 34; 98 F. 2d. 49 (2 Cir., 1938); interview with Mr. Aaron Danzig, April 12, 1978; Claytor interview, July 11, 1978.

81. Notes 68, 73, 74.

82. Stone to Frankfurter, April 29, 1938; Frankfurter to Stone, May 9, 1938; located in Box 171, F17, Frankfurter papers, manuscript division, HLS.

83. Freyer, *Forums of Order,* Ch. VIII enlarges upon this theme.

84. Notes 14–17.

85. Pepper, *Autobiography,* 53–54, states that his essay agrees substantially with Justice Reed's concurrance.

86. Notes 70–72.

87. Ibid., 72. Italics added.

88. Brandeis' undated memoranda written in response to Butler's dissent, 107-8 (italics addes.). Note 72, and note 55 for full cite to Brandeis papers.

89. Note 35.

90. Brandeis, *Business—A Profession,* 337, 339–40; *Letters of Louis D. Brandeis* (Urofsky and Levy eds.;), I, III.

91. Note 7, reference to letters in Urofsky manuscript, 124½, 125½.

92. Notes 31–34, 38. See also Edward A. Purcell, Jr., *The Crisis of Democratic Theory: Scientific Naturalism & the Problem of Value* (Lexington, 1973), 74–94, 59–178.

CHAPTER IV

1. Philip B. Kurland, "Mr. Justice Frankfurter, the Supreme Court, and the *Erie* Doctrine in Diversity Cases," *The Yale Law Journal* LXVII (December 1957), 188–204; Martin H. Redish and Carter G. Phillips, *"Erie* and the Rules of Decision Act: in Search of the Appropriate Dilemma" *Harvard Law Review* 91 (December 1977), 374. William F. Baxter, "Choice of Law and the Federal System," *Stanford Law Review* XVI (1963), 32–33. Harold W. Horwitz, "Toward a Federal Common Law of Choice of Law," *U.C.L.A. Law Review* XIV (1967), 1191–1209. Grant Gilmore, *The Ages of American Law* (New Haven, 1977), 93–95. Henry J. Friendly, "In Praise of *Erie*—And of the New Federal Common Law," *New York University Law Review* XXXIX (May 1964), 405–406. Arthur L. Corbin, "The Laws of the Several States,"

Yale Law Journal L (February 1941), 762–778; Charles E. Clark, "State Law in Federal Courts: The Brooding Omnipresence of *Erie* v. *Tompkins*," *Yale Law Journal* LV (February 1946), 290. David Cavers, *The Choice of Law Process* (Boston, 1965), 64; Robert A. Leflar, *American Conflicts Law* (Charlottesville, 1977).

2. FF to Harlan Fiske Stone, 9 May 1938, Box 171, F. 17, Felix Frankfurter Papers, Manuscript Division, Harvard Law School Library.

3. *Fidelity Union Trust Co.* v. *Field*, 311 U.S. 169 (1940); see also *West* v. *American Tel. & Tel. Co., Six Companies of California* v. *Joint Hwy. Dist. No. 13*, 311 U.S. 180 (1940). The departure from this strict adherence to *Erie* was represented by *Bernhardt* v. *Polygraphic Co. of America*, 350 U.S. 198 (1956) and *King* v. *Order of United Commercial Travelers of America*, 333 U.S. 153 (1948). Mr. Justice Frankfurter was instrumental in this change; see Kurland, cited above. *Klaxon Co.* v. *Stentor Elec. Mfg. Co.*, 313 U.S. 487 (1941); *Day & Zimmerman, Inc.* v. *Challoner*, 423 U.S. 3 (1975). *Ruhlin* v. *New York Life Ins. Co.* 304 U.S. 202 (1938); *Guaranty Trust Co.* v. *York*, 326 U.S. 99 (1945). See also note 2. Redish and Phillips, "*Erie* and the Rules of Decision Act," *HLR* 91 (Dec. 1977), 384–96. See also *Byrd* v. *Blue Ridge Rural Elec. Co-o-, Inc.*, 365 U.S. 525 (1957). *Hanna* v. *Plumer* 380 U.S. 460, 473–74. *Hinderlider* v. *La Plata River & Cherry Creek Ditch Co.*, 304 U.S. 92 (1938); *Clearfield Trust Co.* v. *U.S.* 363 (1943); *Phreibe & Sons, Inc.* v. *U.S.* 332 U.S. 407 (1947); *Association of Westinghouse Salaried Employees* v. *Westinghouse Elec. Corp.* 348 U.S. 437 (1955); *Textile Workers* v. *Lincoln Mills*, 353 U.S. 448 (1957); *Local 174, Teamsters* v. *Lucas Flour Co.*, 369 U.S. 95 (1962); *Smith* v. *Evening News Ass'n.*, 371 U.S. 195 (1966); *International Assoc. of Machinists* v. *Central Airlines, Inc.*, 372 U.S. 682 (1963); *New York Times Co.* v. *Sullivan*, 376 U.S. 254 (1964); *Illinois* v. *Milwaukee*, 406 U.S. 91, 107 (1972). *Diversity Jurisdiction, Hearings on S. 1876 Before the Subcomm. on Improvements in Judicial Machinery of the Senate Comm. on the Judiciary*, 92d Cong. 1st Sess. 162 (Washington 1971), Part 1. I am indebted to David Cavers for this reference. "Suggestions for Improving the Process of Civil Litigation in the Federal Courts to the Chief Justice of the United States" (June 30, 1971), 30; Paul Nejelski; "State-Federal Relations: A Progress Report" (February 9, 1973), 1–2. I am indebted to Robert A. Leflar for these references. See also Shapiro, "Federal Diversity Jurisdiction: A Survey and a Proposal," *HLR* 91 (December 1977), 317–355. Henry J. Friendly, "The Federal Courts," in *American Law: The Third Century, The Law Bicentennial Volume* (Bernard Schwartz ed., New York, 1976), 200–201. For quote from Hart see "The Place of the Federal Courts in the Constitutional Plan," unfinished typed and hand written manuscript," c. 1954, 4, 20, 35, 40, located in Box 24-4, Hart, manuscript division, HLS. As far as I know this essay was never published. I am indebted to Mrs. Erika Chadbourn for bringing it to my attention. See also, Crosskey, *Politics and the Constitution*, I, 363–562, 17–292, 620–674; II, 1165–1166. Of course it was Crosskey who demonstrated the inadequacy of Charles Warren's interpretation of the original drafts of section 34, discussed above. David L. Shapiro, "Federal Diversity Jurisdiction: A Survey and a Proposal," *HLR* 91 (December 1977), 318. Friendly, "In Praise of *Erie*," *NYULR*, XXXIX (May, 1964), 383–422; Arthur J. Keeffe, "In Praise of Joseph Story, *Swift* v. *Tyson* and 'The' True National Common Law," *American University Law Review* XVIII (March 1969), 316–371; John H. Ely, "The Irrepressible Myth of *Erie*," *Harvard Law Review* LXXXVII (June 1974), 1682–1688; Redish and Phillips, "*Erie* and the Rules of Decision Act," *HLR*, 91 (December 1977), 356–401.

4. Alpheus Thomas Mason, *Harlan Fiske Stone: Pillar of the Law*, (New York, 1956), 387–388, 418–419, 457–549, 550–555 and 490–494, 551, 780–781 for

Stone's views on enlargement of federal regulatory authority and the connection of this to his concern for personal rights.

5. Ibid., 512–517, especially 515. For dissent in the flag salute case see 524–534. Citations are *U.S.* v. *Carolene Products Co.*, 304 U.S. 144 (1938); *Minersville School Dist.* v. *Gobitis,* 310 U.S. 586 (1940).

INDEX

United States v. *Caroline Products Co.,* 163
United States v. *Coolidge,* 2, 27
United States v. *Crosby,* 28
Universal law. *See* General law
Upshur, Abel, 18–19, 36, 40, 41

Van Reimsdyke v. *Kane,* 32–33

Wallace, H. B., 47
Wallace, John William, 19, 39, 40, 41, 47, 73, 93
Walsh, Thomas J., 109

Warren, Charles, 105, 111–113, 134–153 passim
Watson v. *Tarpley,* 51–55, 59, 62, 72, 74, 85
Wayman v. *Southard,* 36
Wayne, Justice James, 49
Wharton, Francis, 89, 91, 97
Wheaton, Henry, 27
Williamson v. *Berry,* 49, 51
Wilson, Woodrow, 112
Withers v. *Greene,* 49

Yates v. *Milwaukee,* 57–58, 60
Yntema, Hessel E., 118, 152